Beyond Shallow Faith

Cultivating Christian Maturity
(Ephesians 4:13-15)

by Don Davidson, B.A., J.D.

CFT Publishing

Bedford, Texas

Published by CFT Publishing
Bedford, Texas
ISBN978-0-9992335-2-8

You can contact Don via email at: *donatty@flash.net.*

To read Don's blog, and for more information on Don's writings, including some that are available for free, visit *dondavidson.net.*

If you like this book, you should read Don's first book: *Beyond Blind Faith: Reasons for the Hope We Have (1 Peter 3:15),* which is available on Amazon.com.

TABLE OF CONTENTS

Preface

I primarily rely upon two rules when interpreting scripture. The first is one I borrowed from the law—the doctrine of *pari materia* (Latin for "on the same subject"). This rule recognizes that lawmakers do not intentionally pass laws that contradict each other, and therefore an interpretation which leads to that result is probably wrong. This doctrine requires courts to interpret laws so that they are consistent with each other whenever possible, so long as they address the same general subject or have the same general purpose.

A similar approach will serve us well in biblical interpretation, since we can be reasonably certain that the New Testament writers did not intend to contradict themselves or each other. Because I believe that those authors honestly reported what they knew or believed to be true, I make every effort to reconcile scriptures that appear to be in conflict.

The second rule I follow is that every verse should be interpreted in light of the context in which it appears. What was the author's main point? Who was his audience? In some cases, when and where was the book written? What do the verses preceding and following that verse talk about? We will get much closer to a verse's true meaning if we understand the context in which it appears.

For those who wish to delve deeper, I have provided abundant endnotes, many of which list additional biblical authority for my key points. Like a good parent or teacher, God often repeats himself on important matters to make sure his message is heard and understood, so I usually found multiple verses that furnish corroboration for, and/or clarification of, the theological topics I discuss. So if you want to be like the Bereans and examine the scriptures to see if the things I say are really so (Acts 17:11), I have tried to make it a bit easier for you.

All biblical quotations in this book are from the New American Standard Bible translation. *Italics* are in the original, and indicate that the word is implied in—but not literally part of—the original Greek, Aramaic, or Hebrew. ALL-CAPS are also in the original, and indicate quotations from the Old Testament.

Introduction

In Ephesians 4:14-15, Paul tells us that we as Christians "are no longer to be children, tossed here and there by waves and carried about by every wind of doctrine, by the trickery of men, by craftiness in deceitful scheming; but speaking the truth in love, we are to grow up in all aspects into Him who is the head, even Christ." As he says in Ephesians 4:13, we are to become spiritually mature. The author of Hebrews has a similar message for us in Hebrews 5:11-14.

In my experience, some Christians are just looking for "heaven insurance." All they want from Christianity is to know that they will receive eternal life when they die, and they want to pay the lowest possible earthly premium. If that describes you, then this book is definitely *not* for you. But if you are trying to grow in your faith and become more like Jesus—if you are seeking the abundant life Jesus talked about in John 10:10—then you are one of the people I wrote this for.

My goal is to help you "work out your salvation with fear and trembling." (Philippians 2:12) My first book, *Beyond Blind Faith: Reasons For the Hope We Have (1 Peter 3:15)*, covered Christianity 101. It was intended to give you a firm foundation for faith in Christ by demonstrating that Christianity makes sense and is in fact the one true religion.

Now we need to move on to more advanced topics like spiritual growth, forgiveness, pride, judgment, repentance, *agape* love, and grace. We will explore what the Bible teaches about faith and works, free will vs. predestination, and the existence and power of Satan. We will discuss why Jesus had to die, and why universal salvation is not a biblically sound doctrine. We'll explore what the Bible says about the events surrounding the birth and resurrection of Jesus. And just for fun, we'll talk about the many things God orchestrated in order to make planet Earth the ideal spot—perhaps like no other—for life to grow and flourish.

As I stated in my first book, *Beyond Blind Faith*, I am firmly convinced that Christianity is not merely useful, helpful, and/or convenient—it is truth itself. With that in mind, we need to learn as much as possible about God's ways so that we can live as he intended. This book will help those who wish to pursue such knowledge.

Chapter 1
SPIRITUAL GROWTH

The church at Corinth was so messed up that the apostle Paul wrote at least three letters—and probably four—trying to straighten them out.[1] He also made three visits there,[2] and sent Timothy and Titus as well.[3]

The Corinthians had split into four cliques, each revering a different leader: Jesus, Paul, Peter, and Apollos.[4] These factions quarreled with each other,[5] arousing jealousy and strife, arrogance and boasting.[6] Their disputes often spilled over into lawsuits in Rome's civil courts.[7]

Immorality had crept into the church as well. One of its members was engaging in sexual relations with his stepmother,[8] and the other church members bragged about the relationship.[9] Communion had lost its sacred, commemorative purpose, with some even using the occasion to get drunk.[10]

Perhaps worst of all, some of the Corinthians denied Christ's resurrection.[11] Paul pointed out that they were denying the very heart of the Christian message, for

> if Christ has not been raised, your faith is worthless; you are still in your sins. Then those also who have fallen asleep in Christ have perished. If we have hoped in Christ in this life only, we are of all men most to be pitied.
> —1 Corinthians 15:17-19

Paul diagnosed the Corinthians' problem as spiritual immaturity:

> And I, brethren, could not speak to you as to spiritual men, but as to men of flesh, as to infants in Christ. I gave you milk to drink, not solid food; for you were not yet able *to receive it*. Indeed, even now you are not yet able, for you are still fleshly. For since there is jealousy and strife among you, are you not fleshly, and are you not walking like mere men?
>
> —1 Corinthians 3:1-3

The author of Hebrews perceived a similar problem among his intended audience:

> For though by this time you ought to be teachers, you have need again for someone to teach you the elementary principles of the oracles of God, and you have come to need milk and not solid food. For everyone who partakes *only* of milk is not accustomed to the word of righteousness, for he is an infant.
>
> —Hebrews 5:12-13

Their message is clear—we need to grow up spiritually and become mature in our faith. So where will we find the step-by-step guide in the New Testament that explains how we do that?

We won't. It's not there.

Nevertheless, the New Testament authors have not left us clueless. They provided a lot of hints about how to attain spiritual maturity.

Before we explore those hints, we need to recognize that this is a gradual process. Unlike salvation, which happens the instant we commit ourselves to Christ, spiritual growth takes time. Thus, Peter encouraged his readers to "grow in the grace and knowledge of our Lord and Savior Jesus Christ." (2 Peter 3:18) Paul told the Philippians that "He who began a good work in you will perfect it until the day of Christ Jesus." (Philippians 1:6) He also said that "we are to grow up in all *aspects* into Him who is the head, *even* Christ." (Ephesians 4:15) The author of Hebrews indicates that maturity is a matter of practice, the mature Christians being those who "because of practice have their senses trained to discern good and evil." (Hebrews 5:14) Other verses speak of the growth of our faith, our love, and our maturity.[12]

I believe spiritual growth is similar to physical growth in one respect. When you were a child, you never had to tell yourself, "Today I will grow." You needed good nutrition rather than determination. In the same way, if you give yourself the proper spiritual nourishment, you will grow spiritually.

Just to be clear, I am not talking about salvation. Paul and the author of Hebrews chided their readers for immaturity, but their salvation did not appear to be in question. They had simply failed to grow in their faith. Their poor spiritual diet had stunted their spiritual growth.

So what constitutes a good spiritual diet? It begins with Bible study.

Bible study

Knowledge of Scripture gives us a rock solid foundation for our faith which keeps us from being "tossed here and there by waves and carried about by every wind of doctrine, by the trickery of men, by craftiness in deceitful scheming." (Ephesians 4:14) When you have a strong knowledge and understanding of the Bible, no one can deceive you with man-made doctrines.

For example, when you understand that Jesus told us to love others,[13] including even our enemies,[14] and that Paul told us not to judge those outside the church,[15] you won't be misled by those who advocate hatred, bigotry, and intolerance in the name of Christianity.

Jesus understood the importance of knowing the scriptures. When he was tempted by Satan in the wilderness, he quoted scripture to frustrate the devil's efforts.[16] Even when Satan quoted Psalm 91:11-12[17] to argue that God would protect Jesus if he hurled himself off the top of the Temple, Jesus' superior knowledge of Scripture enabled him to counter with Deuteronomy 6:16: "You shall not put the LORD your God to the test."[18] Jesus quoted scripture in many contexts, to both instruct his disciples and refute his opponents.[19]

Paul advised his pupil, Timothy, to "give attention to the *public* reading *of Scripture*, to exhortation and teaching" (1 Timothy 4:13), also reminding him "that from childhood you have known the sacred writings which are able to give you the wisdom that leads to salvation through faith which is in Christ Jesus." (2 Timothy 3:15)

For Paul, an understanding of scripture was vital for becoming a mature Christian: "All Scripture is inspired by God and profitable for teaching, for reproof, for correction, for training in righteousness; so that the man of God may be adequate, equipped for every good work." (2 Timothy 3:16-17)

During Paul's lifetime, in the mid-first century, some of the New Testament books had yet to be written, and many of those that did exist were just beginning to circulate. The only available scripture was often the Old Testament. So these early disciples relied heavily on what they had learned about Jesus from other Christians.

Thus, Paul told Timothy to be "nourished on the words of the faith and of the sound doctrine which you have been following" (1 Timothy 4:6), and to instruct others in the same way: "The things which you have heard from me in the presence of many witnesses, entrust these to faithful men who will be able to teach others also" (2 Timothy 2:2). One of the qualifications for a church leader was that he "[hold] fast the faithful word which is in accordance with the teaching, so that he will be able both to exhort in sound doctrine and to refute those who contradict." (Titus 1:9)[20]

Now we have those "words of the faith" and that "sound doctrine" in the books of the New Testament. As Christians we need to study them and learn from them,[21] because knowledge of scripture promotes spiritual growth.

Prayer

I have not found a single verse in the Bible that says prayer stimulates spiritual growth. Yet I do not doubt that such is the case, for we have so many examples of prayer being an indispensable part of our relationship with God. Jesus prayed,[22] and assumed that his followers would also pray.[23] After Jesus' death and resurrection, his disciples routinely prayed,[24] as did Paul.[25] Indeed, the letters of Paul and others frequently mention prayer by and for the Christian community.[26]

Prayer was part of Jewish life as well. Abraham, Isaac, and Jacob all prayed,[27] as did Moses.[28] 2 Samuel 21:14 and

Beyond Shallow Faith

24:25 speak of the Lord being "moved by prayer." Even King David, the man after God's own heart,[29] prayed.[30]

Shall we ignore "so great a cloud of witnesses" (Hebrews 12:1) who gave us the example of prayer? We do so at our peril. Perhaps you can be a Christian without prayer, but I am confident you will stunt your spiritual growth by doing so.

Other Spiritual Nourishment

Like many children, I hated vegetables when I was young. But my parents made me eat them because they were "good for you." As I grew I learned to like them—at least, most of them. That is how I regard some spiritual habits that help us grow: giving, service, fellowship, worship, and obedience. They nourish our spirits by cultivating the bond we have with God and each other, and by weaning us from the charms and enticements of the world. Like vegetables, these spiritual habits may not seem very tasty in the beginning—at least, in my experience—but they become easier and more enjoyable the more we practice them. And they are indeed good for us.

Giving. Cain and Abel, the sons of Adam and Eve, recognized the importance of giving back to God.[31] Jacob promised to give God one-tenth of all that he received.[32] The Lord later made tithes and offerings mandatory in the Law,[33] and scolded his people through Malachi the prophet for their failure to comply with this requirement.[34]

In the New Testament we have many examples of people giving because of their faith in God: the Magi who brought gifts to the baby Jesus and his parents;[35] the poor widow whom Jesus praised for giving all she had to live on;[36] the women who supported Jesus' ministry from their own resources;[37] the Christians in Jerusalem who shared with their brothers and sisters;[38] the Philippians who supported Paul's ministry;[39] and the churches in Syria and Greece who sent money for the poor in Jerusalem.[40]

Giving teaches us to find our joy and contentment in God rather than in material possessions.[41] Giving focuses us on others rather than ourselves. Giving also demonstrates the sincerity of our faith and love.[42] Besides, "God loves a cheerful giver." (2 Corinthians 9:7)

Service. Giving is not limited to financial generosity. The Second Greatest Commandment is to love our neighbor as ourselves,[43] for Jesus told us to "love one another." (John 13:34)[44] A necessary corollary is that we are to serve one another.[45] Jesus said those who wish to be great must serve, just as he came to serve.[46]

So we must give of our time and our talents in addition to our money—to God and his church, of course, but also to "the least of these." (Matthew 25:40 and 25:45) And like the good and faithful servants in Jesus' parable of the talents, [47] serving matures us and prepares us for greater responsibilities. This is surely what Paul meant when he said:

> And He gave some as apostles, and some as prophets, and some as evangelists, and some as pastors and teachers, for the equipping of the saints for the work of service, to the building up of the body of Christ; until we all attain to the unity of the faith, and of the knowledge of the Son of God, to a mature man, to the measure of the stature which belongs to the fullness of Christ.
>
> —Ephesians 4:11-13

9

Beyond Shallow Faith

Fellowship and Corporate Worship. God never meant for us to struggle with our faith by ourselves. Early in Jesus' ministry, he chose twelve men to share his journey.[48] He sent them out to preach and to heal in pairs, not alone.[49] He followed the same practice when he sent the seventy.[50]

Togetherness was an essential part of the early Christian experience, as we read in verses such as Acts 2:1 ("they were all together in one place"), Acts 4:31 ("when they had prayed, the place where they had gathered together was shaken"), and Acts 12:12 ("he went to the house of Mary . . . where many were gathered together and were praying").[51] Acts 2:42 tells us that after Pentecost the new Christians "were continually devoting themselves to the apostles' teaching and to fellowship, to the breaking of bread and to prayer."

Sharing our knowledge makes all of us smarter. Sharing our faith makes all of us more confident. Sharing our love makes all of us more compassionate.

The author of Hebrews recognized this power of fellowship and corporate worship when he said:

> Let us consider how to stimulate one another to love and good deeds, not forsaking our own assembling together, as is the habit of some, but encouraging *one another*; and all the more as you see the day drawing near.
>
> —Hebrews 10:24-25

Paul made a similar point in Romans 1:11-12:

> For I long to see you so that I may impart some spiritual gift to you, that you may be established; that is, that I may be encouraged to-

gether with you while among you, each of us by the other's faith, both yours and mine.[52]

Spiritual growth is like tennis: you can learn to play the game by yourself, but you will learn faster, and become much more skilled at it, if you play with others—including those who have played the game longer, and play it better, than you do. You will improve even faster if you have instructors who can teach you the finer points of the game. Similarly, you might be able to grow spiritually without help from anyone but Jesus, but you will grow faster and get further by drawing on the wisdom and experience of other Christians.

Obedience. None of us can attain perfection in this life. So when I talk of obedience, I do not mean that we must become sinless. But if we want to grow into mature Christians, we must at least strive for perfection, for nothing will stunt our spiritual growth more than deliberate disobedience of God's commands.

Jesus was not shy about demanding that we pursue righteousness. He told us to "be perfect, as your heavenly Father is perfect." (Matthew 5:48) He warned that "unless your righteousness surpasses *that* of the scribes and Pharisees, you will not enter the kingdom of heaven." (Matthew 5:20) He also said that those who "hunger and thirst for righteousness" are blessed—and that "they shall be satisfied." (Matthew 5:6) When he told us not to worry about food or clothing, he added: "But seek first His kingdom and His righteousness, and all these things will be added to you." (Matthew 6:33)

Paul, that champion of salvation by faith, also encouraged righteous behavior. He did not do so because righteousness saves, but because it helps us grow. In chapter four of Ephesians—the same chapter in which he told us not to be "children . . . carried about by every wind of doctrine" (Ephesians 4:14)—he added detailed instructions on how we are to behave, warning against sensuality (v. 19), lying (v. 25), and stealing (v. 28), among other sins. You will find similar lists of behaviors to avoid in Mark 7:20-23, Romans 1:28-31, Galatians 5:19-21, 1 Timothy 6:3-5, Titus 3:3, and 1 Peter 2:1-3. The New Testament authors must have thought obedience to God's commands was important since they emphasized it repeatedly.

Conclusion

Some Christians today do not seem that much different from those immature people who received the letter we now call First Corinthians. Too often we see disputes within churches where there should be love and unity. Nor is it unusual to hear of Christians committing adultery or getting divorced.[53] I am particularly saddened when I hear Christians spewing bile and hatred toward those of a different race, color, creed, nationality, or sexual orientation.

These are all signs of spiritual immaturity. I do not say that these people will not be saved, for that is not my decision. But I do wish they would grow up.

Endnotes for Chapter One, "Spiritual Growth"

1. 1 Corinthians was Paul's second letter to the Corinthians. We do not have the prior letter, but Paul refers to it in 1 Corinthians 5:9. 2 Corinthians 2:3-4 and 7:8 talk about another letter, apparently written after 1 Corinthians, making a total of four letters Paul wrote to that church.

2. See 2 Corinthians 7:6-7, 12:14, and 13:1-2.

3. 1 Corinthians 4:17 and 16:10-11; 2 Corinthians 8:16-23 and 12:18

4. 1 Corinthians 1:12-13 and 11:18-19. Apollos is also mentioned in Acts 18:24, 19:1; 1 Corinthians 3:4-6, 3:22, 4:6, 16:12; and Titus 3:13.

5. 1 Corinthians 1:11

6. 1 Corinthians 3:3, 3:21, and 4:6-7

7. 1 Corinthians 6:1-8

8. 1 Corinthians 5:1

9. See 1 Corinthians 5:6: "Your boasting is not good." Paul does not tell us why the Corinthians boasted about this affair. Perhaps the offending church member was wealthy or prestigious.

10. 1 Corinthians 11:20-22

11. 1 Corinthians 15:12

12. See, for example: 2 Corinthians 10:15; Colossians 2:7; 2 Thessalonians 1:3; Hebrews 6:1. Similarly, see 1 Peter 2:2, 2:5, and 2 Peter 1:8.

13. See for example: Matthew 19:19; Luke 10:26-37; John 13:34-35; Galatians 5:14; and 1 John 2:9-11, 3:23, 4:7-12.

14. Matthew 5:44; Luke 6:27, 6:35

15. 1 Corinthians 5:12; see also Romans 14:10-13. Jesus also told us not to judge others. See, for example, Matthew 7:1-5 and Luke 6:37-42.

16. See Matthew 4:1-11 and Luke 4:1-13.

17. Psalm 91:11-12 says:

> For He will give His angels charge concerning you,
> To guard you in all your ways.
> They will bear you up in their hands,
> That you do not strike your foot against a stone.

18. See Matthew 4:6-7 and Luke 4:9-12. The full quote from Deuteronomy 6:16 is: "You shall not put the LORD your God to the test, as you tested *Him* at Massah." Massah refers to Exodus 17:1-7, when the people grumbled about a lack of water to drink, and the Lord gave them water from a rock. Massah is also known as Rephidim and Meribah. See Exodus 17:1 and 17:7.

19. See, for example: Matthew 4:4, 4:7, 4:10, 5:27, 5:31, 5:33, 5:35, 5:38, 5:43, 7:23, 9:13, 11:5, 11:10, 12:40, 13:14-15, 15:4, 15:7-9, 16:27, 18:16, 19:4-5, 19:18-19, 21:13, 21:16, 21:42, 22:31-32, 22:37-39, 22:43-44, 23:39, 24:29-30, 26:31, 27:46; Mark 7:6-7, 7:10, 8:18, 9:48, 10:6-8, 12:10-11, 12:26, 12:29-31, 12:36, 13:14, 13:24-26, 14:27, 14:62; Luke 4:4, 4:8, 4:12, 4:18-21, 7:27, 13:27, 13:35, 18:20, 19:46, 20:17, 20:37, 20:42-43, 21:27, 22:37, 22:69, 23:30, 23:46, 24:25-27 (by implication), 24:44-47 (by implication); John 7:38, 10:34, 13:18

20. See also Titus 2:1: "But as for you, speak the things which are fitting for sound doctrine."

21. If you are a beginner at Bible study, here are a few suggestions:

1. Feel free to begin slowly, but begin, and do it every day. When I was a baby Christian, I set aside five minutes a day to read and study the Bible. Soon five minutes was not enough, so I raised it to ten, then fifteen, and so on.

2. Use other resources to help you. I have found Bible commentaries to be very useful in understanding the meaning and context of difficult verses. And abundant articles are available on the internet on virtually any biblical topic.

3. Take copious notes. I like to summarize the portion of the Bible I am studying, and then add comments later from other sources. Taking notes will help you remember what you have read, and you will have a source to come back to when you need it. I use a computer so I can easily access my notes and make needed additions and changes.

22. Matthew 14:23, 19:13, 26:36-44; Mark 1:35, 6:46, 14:32-39; Luke 3:21, 5:16, 6:12, 9:18, 9:28-29, 11:1, 22:32, 22:41-45; John 11:41-42, 17:1-26; Hebrews 5:7

23. Matthew 5:44, 6:5-13, 21:22, 24:20, 26:41; Mark 11:24-25, 13:18, 14:38; Luke 6:28, 11:2-4, 18:1, 21:36, 22:40, 22:46

24. Acts 1:14, 1:24, 2:42, 4:24-31, 6:4, 6:6, 8:14-15, 9:40, 10:9, 11:4-5, 12:5, 12:12, 13:3

25. Acts 9:11, 14:23 (with Barnabas), 16:25 (with Silas), 20:36, 21:5 (with the disciples at Tyre), 22:17, 28:8; Romans 1:10, 8:26 (by implication), 10:1, 14:14-15; 2 Corinthians 12:8, 13:7, 13:9; Ephesians 1:16; Philippians 1:4, 1:9; Colossians 1:3, 1:9; 1 Thessalonians 1:2, 3:10; 2 Thessalonians 1:11; 2 Timothy 1:3; Philemon 1:4

26. Romans 12:12, 15:30-32; 1 Corinthians 7:5, 11:4-5, 11:13, 14:13; 2 Corinthians 1:11, 9:14; Ephesians 6:18-19; Philippians 1:19, 4:6; Colossians 4:2-3; 1 Thessalonians 5:17, 5;25; 2 Thessalonians 3:1; 1 Timothy 2:1, 2:8, 4:5, 5:5; Philemon 1:22; Hebrews 13:18; James 5:13-16; 1 Peter 3:7, 4:7; 3 John 1:2; Jude 1:20; and see Revelation 5:8, 8:3-4

27. Genesis 20:7, 20:17, 25:21, 32:11

28. Numbers 11:2; Deuteronomy 9:20, 9:26

29. 1 Samuel 13:14

30. 2 Samuel 7:18-29, 15:31

31. Genesis 4:3-4

32. Genesis 28:22

33. For example, tithes are addressed in Leviticus 27:30-33, Numbers 18:21-32, and Deuteronomy 14:22. Offerings are covered in many locations throughout Leviticus, Numbers, and Deuteronomy. Offerings included burnt offerings, sin offerings, guilt offerings, peace offerings, grain offerings, drink offerings, wave offerings, freewill offerings, thanksgiving offerings, and first fruits. The Israelite community made daily offerings, Sabbath offerings, monthly offerings, and offerings on special occasions such as Passover, Day of Atonement, the Feast of Unleavened Bread, the Feast of Weeks, and the Feast of Booths.

34. Malachi 3:8-10

35. Matthew 2:11

36. Mark 12:41-44 and Luke 21:1-4

37. Luke 8:2-3; see also Matthew 27:55 and Mark 15:40-41

38. Acts 2:44-45

39. Philippians 4:15-18

40. See Acts 11:27-30, Romans 15:25-27, 1 Corinthians 16:1-3, and 2 Corinthians 8:1-15 and 9:1-7.

41. See Philippians 4:11: "I have learned to be content in whatever circumstances I am." See also 1 Timothy 6:6 and Hebrews 13:5.

42. 2 Corinthians 8:8 and 8:24

43. Leviticus 19:18; Matthew 19:19, 22:36; Galatians 5:14

44. See also John 13:35, 15:12, 15:17; and see 1 John 3:11, 3:23 and 2 John 5

45. Galatians 5:13

46. Matthew 20:25-28; Mark 9:35, 10:41-45; Luke 22:24-27

47. See Matthew 25:14-23 and Luke 19:12-19.

48. See Mark 3:13-19 and Luke 6:12-16.

49. Mark 6:7

50. Luke 10:1

51. See also, Acts 1:15, 2:44-46, 14:27, 15:6, 15:30, and 20:7-8.

52. See also Philippians 1:27, where Paul urged the Philippians to stand firm "in one spirit, with one mind striving together for the faith of the gospel. . . ." And in 2 Timothy 2:22 he gave this advice: "Now flee from youthful lusts and pursue righteousness, faith, love and peace, with those who call on the Lord from a pure heart."

53. Jesus was clear that divorce for any reason other than adultery was not sanctioned by God. See Matthew 5:31-32 and 19:9, Mark 10:11-12, and Luke 16:18. Paul said something similar in 1 Corinthians 7:10-16.

Chapter 2
SHARING HEAVEN

The New Testament talks a lot about mercy and forgiveness. I don't just mean the mercy and forgiveness that we hope to receive from God, but also the mercy and forgiveness that God insists that we show toward others.

For example, Jesus warns us that we must forgive others if we expect to receive mercy from God: "For if you forgive others for their transgressions, your heavenly Father will also forgive you. But if you do not forgive others, then your Father will not forgive your transgressions." (Matthew 6:14-15)[1] In one of Jesus' parables, an unforgiving servant is punished by his master for enforcing a small debt after being forgiven a very large debt.[2] The Lord's Prayer asks God to forgive our debts," as we also have forgiven our debtors." (Matthew 6:12)[3] Indeed, we are to forgive repeatedly:

> Then Peter came and said to Him, "Lord, how often shall my brother sin against me and I forgive him? Up to seven times?" Jesus said to him, "I do not say to you, up to seven times, but up to seventy times seven."
>
> —Matthew 18:21-22[4]

A closely related concept is that of *peace*. Jesus urged us to "be at peace with one another" (Mark 9:50), while Paul went even further: "If possible, so far as it depends on you, be at peace with all men." (Romans 12:18)[5] Other New Testament writers agree.[6] Peace requires forgiveness, because we cannot be at peace with someone against whom we harbor a grudge.

Beyond Shallow Faith

So what do forgiveness, mercy, and peace have to do with Heaven? To answer this question, let's consider what the New Testament tells us about Heaven. Aside from the spectacular descriptions in Revelation chapters 21 and 22,[7] which may have symbolic meanings, the Bible tells us little about what Heaven will be like. As you would expect, God is there, and the Lord's Prayer implies that in Heaven his will prevails.[8] We know that those who are accepted into Heaven will receive eternal life.[9] Our mortal bodies will somehow be replaced by, or transformed into, an immortal form, and we will always be with the Lord.[10] Hunger and thirst will no longer exist,[11] and people will not get married anymore.[12] Yet these verses tell us surprisingly little about what we will actually experience in Heaven.

Other New Testament verses speak of treasure and reward,[13] but these ambiguous terms only hint at the wonders in store for us. Similarly, Jesus' other references to Heaven—for example that a rich man will have difficulty getting in,[14] or that Heaven rejoices over one repentant sinner[15]—reveal nothing about what we can expect to find there.

Paul is only slightly more enlightening when he tells us that "now we see in a mirror dimly, but then face to face; now I know in part, but then I will know fully just as I also have been fully known" (1 Corinthians 13:12), or when he implies that the glory of Heaven will make us forget all about our sufferings in this life.[16] His description of being "caught up into Paradise" where he "heard inexpressible words, which a man is not permitted to speak" (2 Corinthians 12:4) sounds amazing, but doesn't even suggest what he saw and heard there.

Of the New Testament writers, John may provide the most helpful insight. For example, while discussing the mystery surrounding eternal life, he gives us an important clue about Heaven:

> Beloved, now we are children of God, and it has not appeared as yet what we will be. We know that when He appears, we will be like Him, because we will see Him just as He is.
>
> —1 John 3:2

When John says "we will be like Him," does he mean that we will have Christ's compassionate and forgiving nature? I believe so, because John insists that hatred is inconsistent with true Christianity.[17] Yet I think the most revealing description of Heaven is in two verses from John's Revelation:

> And I heard a loud voice from the throne, saying, "Behold, the tabernacle of God is among men, and He will dwell among them, and they shall be His people, and God Himself will be among them, and He will wipe away every tear from their eyes; and there will no longer be *any* death; there will no longer be *any* mourning, or crying, or pain; the first things have passed away."
>
> —Revelation 21:3-4[18]

In John's eyes, Heaven will be a place of perfect peace and harmony, where everyone will get along together, and people will no longer hurt one another. Crying and pain, like death, will be banished. The causes of suffering in this life will be abolished.

But how can any of this occur without forgiveness?

How can Heaven be a place of joy, contentment, and delightful relationships if our enmity is allowed to intrude?

Could God possibly tolerate rancor in Heaven? I do not believe he can.

Our hostility would contaminate Paradise, because bitterness, resentment, cruelty, and emotional pain would inevitably follow. Heaven is simply not big enough for both us and our animosity. For Heaven to be Heaven, peace and forgiveness must reign supreme. If we are unwilling to forgive our enemies, we will find it impossible to share Heaven with them.

Is there anyone you don't *want* God to forgive? Maybe she was unfaithful or unkind. Maybe he committed a terrible crime against you or someone you love, or simply betrayed your trust. Whoever he is, and whatever she may have done, you must try to forgive them. After all, if they repent and ask God for forgiveness, they may already be in Heaven when you get there.

Don't deceive yourself into thinking God couldn't possibly forgive that person. Jesus is very forgiving. He forgave the men who were crucifying him.[19] He forgave one of the two criminals who were executed beside him.[20] Christ stands ready to forgive all who will repent and surrender their lives to him—and that includes the person you may not want him to forgive.[21]

I understand that forgiveness can be hard, and I don't know that we can perfectly forgive others in this life because of our flawed human nature. But I believe we must try, because Jesus wants us to—and because Jesus *commands* us to.

However, let us be clear about what forgiveness is and what it is not. Forgiveness is not trust—forgiving the employee who stole from you does not mean that you must rehire that person. Forgiving the wife who cheated on you does not mean you suddenly trust her not to betray you again. Trust takes time to build, or to rebuild, and can be destroyed in an instant. But you can still forgive someone you no longer trust.

Nor does forgiveness mean that I no longer feel the emotional pain that I suffered from the original wrong. Forgiveness in fact has nothing to do with how we *feel*—it has everything to do with how we *act*.

Regardless of how we feel, we must act with love. Forgiveness means that we do not seek revenge. We do not try to get even. We pray for our enemies, and try to show them kindness.[22] We ask God to turn our hostility to love. When we do this, our feelings of anger, hatred, or bitterness will eventually subside.

If we want God to forgive us, we must try to forgive others. And that includes those we find hardest to forgive, because we may have to share Heaven with them.

Beyond Shallow Faith

Endnotes for Chapter Two, "Sharing Heaven"

1. See also Mark 11:25-26.

2. Matthew 18:23-35

3. See also Luke 11:4, Ephesians 4:31-32, Colossians 3:13; and James 2:13.

4. See also Luke 17:3-4.

5. Paul talks elsewhere about the need to be at peace with other men, such as Romans 14:19; 2 Corinthians 13:11; Ephesians 2:14-16 and 4:2-3; 1 Thessalonians 5:13; and Titus 3:2.

6. See, for example, Hebrews 12:14; James 3:18; 1 Peter 3:8.

7. For example, Revelation 21:9-22:5 describes the New Jerusalem as a huge walled city of gold, jasper, pearl, and precious gems, which encloses the tree of life.

8. See Matthew 6:9-10.

9. See Matthew 19:29; Mark 10:30; Luke 18:29-30; John 3:14-16, 3:36, 4:14, 5:24, 6:27, 6:40, 6:47, 6:54, 10:27-28, 12:25, 17:1-3; Acts 13:46-48; Romans 2:7, 5:21, 6:22-23; 2 Corinthians 5:1; Galatians 6:8; 1 Timothy 1:16, 6:12; Titus 1:2, 3:7; 1 John 2:25, 5:11-13, 5:20; Jude 21.

10. 1 Corinthians 15:42-54; 2 Corinthians 5:1-4; Philippians 3:20-21; 1 Thessalonians 4:13-17; 1 Peter 1:3-4

11. Revelation 7:16

12. Matthew 22:29-30; Mark 12:24-25

13. Matthew 5:11-12, 6:20-21, 19:21; Mark 10:21; Luke 6:22-23, 12:33-34, 18:22; 1 Corinthians 3:8, 2 Corinthians 4:17-18, 1 Timothy 6:19, Hebrews 10:35; Revelation 22:12

14. Matthew 19:23-26; Mark 10:25

15. Luke 15:7, 15:10

16. See Romans 8:18.

17. 1 John 2:9; see also 1 John 2:11, 3:10, 3:15, 4:20

18. See also Revelation 7:17.

19. Luke 23:33-34

20. Luke 23:32-33 and 23:39-43

21. For example, see John 3:15-18.

22. Matthew 5:44; Luke 6:27, 35; Romans 12:20

Chapter 3
THE BIGGEST OBSTACLETO REAL HAPPINESS

I believe one sin[1] causes God more sadness than any other. I am not referring to blasphemy against the Holy Spirit—the so-called "unforgivable" sin[2]—for I suspect very few souls are jeopardized by that particular offense. Nor am I talking about murder, torture, or any sexual misbehavior.

As awful as those are, their impact is dwarfed by another transgression, which is both far more pervasive and far more harmful, when viewed from God's perspective. That transgression infects all of us to some degree, and keeps us from enjoying the relationship that is the purpose of our existence, while also jeopardizing our chance for eternal life. I speak of pride.

I am *not* talking about pride in the sense of positive self-esteem, justified confidence in one's own abilities, or the satisfaction of a job well done.

I mean the haughty pride that deludes us into believing that human knowledge and achievement have no limits. I mean the conceit that convinces us that our ancestors were all superstitious idiots and morons, and that their stories and their values are worthless drivel. I mean the arrogance that tells us that we don't need God because we are doing quite well without him, while ignoring the inevitability of death and decay.

God wants us to have happiness, peace, and contentment in this life, as well as eternal life after we die. But our pride blinds us to this truth. Because of pride, many people seek happiness through their own efforts—money, possessions, power, fame, drugs, alcohol, marriage, sex, children, etc.—and come to God, if at all, only after realizing that these things ultimately do not satisfy. Indeed, they *cannot* satisfy, because they do not last. Real happiness requires that for which we were created: a loving relationship with our Heavenly Father.

Pride is the biggest obstacle to that relationship because our pride, more than any other sin, keeps us apart from God by persuading us that we don't need him. We don't need his rules, because we can make our own decisions about right and wrong. We don't need his help, because we are independent and self-reliant.

Pride builds barriers between us and God by directing our focus toward ourselves rather than him. In short, pride pushes and pulls us away from him.

Pride often came between men and God in the Bible.[3] The psalmist knew this truth:

> The wicked, in the haughtiness of his counten-
> ance, does not seek *Him*.
> All his thoughts are, "There is no God."
> —Psalms 10:4[4]

Moses warned the Israelites not to become proud and forget about God.[5] Yet the people repeatedly did exactly that. After Solomon's kingdom split, the pride of the people of the northern kingdom of Israel[6] led them to abandon their faith. God, speaking through the prophet Hosea, said of them:

> As *they had* their pasture, they became satisfied,
> And being satisfied, their heart became proud;
> Therefore they forgot Me.
> —Hosea 13:6[7]

Beyond Shallow Faith

More than one-hundred years later, in the time of the prophet Jeremiah, the residents of the southern kingdom of Judah made the same mistake. Because of their haughtiness, which led them into idolatry and wickedness, the Lord said they were worthless and threatened them with captivity if they did not humble themselves.[8] They didn't, and the seventy-year exile in Babylon resulted.

In Jesus' time, many wicked people flocked to him and to John the Baptist, seeking and finding forgiveness.[9] But the Jewish religious leaders rejected Jesus. Their pride would not let them consider the possibility that someone with such a humble background—one who was so very different from themselves—could be God's Messiah.[10] They refused to believe that this carpenter from Galilee knew more about God than they did. So they missed their Messiah.

God wants to have a relationship with each of us. He created us for that purpose. But to get there, we need to acknowledge that he is God *and that we are not*. We must come to him in humility, recognizing that he knows more than we do about what is best for us. The Bible praises this kind of humility,[11] just as it denounces arrogant pride.[12] Jesus and Paul both exemplified this attribute of humility.[13] Many Old Testament characters—some of whom were guilty of grievous offenses—received God's favor and mercy by humbling themselves before him: for example, David,[14] Ahab,[15] Josiah,[16] Rehoboam,[17] Hezekiah,[18] and Manasseh.[19] Jesus often spoke of the importance of humility and the dangers of pride.[20]

When we humble ourselves and surrender to God, we put ourselves in his hands, trusting that he knows, and will do, what is best for us. Thus, we give him control of our lives—and frankly, a lot of us don't want to give up that control. We prize our independence so highly that many people do not even recognize pride as a problem. They confuse it with self-confidence or emotional strength, while they ridicule humility as a character trait of the weak.

People who commit sins that hurt others usually *know* they've done wrong. The prideful seldom do. This fact distinguishes pride from almost all other sins. Arrogant people embrace the very evil which separates them from God—and they are happy to do so, because they see nothing wrong with it.

This makes pride extremely pernicious. Of all the evils in the world, pride is the one most responsible for keeping us apart from God. As a result, we miss out on the abundant life we could experience here on earth, and we risk losing the chance for eternal life, both of which must cause God immense sorrow.

However, the destructiveness of pride does not stop there, because pride is also one of the most common of all evils. It afflicts all of us to some degree. Because of pride, the most difficult words to say in any language are: "I was wrong" and "I'm sorry." When we do something we know is wrong, pride tells us to justify our conduct by blaming someone else, by claiming that "everyone does it," or by focusing on some worthwhile goal that we believe justifies our conduct. Thus, our pride overrules our very real need to admit our faults and to ask for forgiveness from the people we love—*and from God.*

To find real happiness, we need to cultivate the loving relationship our Creator wants to have with us. And to do that, we must overcome our pride, which is the biggest obstacle to that relationship. We must humble ourselves, admit our failures, ask him for forgiveness, and submit ourselves to his authority. He, in turn, will love us, care for us, comfort us, and grant us eternal life. And ironically, he will also exalt us: "Humble yourselves in the presence of the Lord, and He will exalt you." (James 4:10)[21]

Ch. 3 – The Biggest Obstacle to Real Happiness

Endnotes for Chapter Three, "The Biggest Obstacle to Real Happiness"

1. The Greek word for "sin" is *hamartia,* which means "a missing of the mark"—the "mark" being God's will or God's law. Simply put, "sin" means to fall short of what God wants us to be. See Romans 3:23.

2. See Matthew 12:31-32, Mark 3:28-29, and Luke 12:10. The nature of this unforgivable sin has been widely (and wildly) debated. I believe a person commits this sin when he or she knows that Christianity is true, yet deliberately and consciously rejects that truth and chooses to live and speak contrary to it. (See, for example, 2 Peter 2:20-22.) In my experience, such people are rare, because the vast majority of those who truly understand, accept, and live the truth of Christianity find such peace and contentment that they would never want to go back to living in darkness again. Thus, those who reject Christianity out of ignorance, misunderstanding, or skepticism—and I have been *all* of those—have not committed the unforgivable sin.

   If you want to give your life to Christ, you can be certain that you have not committed this unforgivable sin. Jesus said, "No one can come to Me unless the Father who sent Me draws him. . . ." (John 6:44) A person who has committed the "unforgivable sin" will no longer be drawn to Christ by the Father.

3. For examples of how pride comes between men and God, see Judges 7:2; 2 Chronicles 32:24-26; Job 35:12; Psalms 20:7-8; Proverbs 30:11-14; Isaiah 10:12-15; Jeremiah 9:23-24, 23:31-32; Ezekiel 16:49-50; Daniel 5:18-23; Malachi 3:13-15; 1 Corinthians 1:26-31, 3:18-21, 8:1-2; 1 Timothy 3:4-6, 6:3-5; 2 Timothy 3:1-4; James 4:4-10; 2 Peter 2:18-19; 1 John 2:15-16.

4. Psalms 10:4

5. Deuteronomy 8:11-14

6. After Solomon's death, his kingdom was divided in two, with the kingdom of Israel in the north, and the kingdom of Judah in the south. See 1 Kings 11:9-13, 12:12-20; 2 Chronicles 10:12-19.

7. Hosea was a prophet to the northern kingdom of Israel during the eighth century B.C. (approximately 770 to 722 B.C.). In 722 B.C., the Assyrians conquered the northern kingdom and dispersed most of its pop-

ulation throughout the Assyrian Empire. Thus, the northern kingdom ceased to exist.

8. See Jeremiah 13:8-10 and 13:15-17. For more on the Babylonian Exile, see my book, *Beyond Blind Faith*, Chapter Three, "Why Do Bad Things Happen (to Me)?," footnote 18.

9. See, for example, Mathew 9:10-13, 11:19, 21:31-32; Mark 2:15-17; Luke 5:29-32, 7:34, 7:36-48, 15:1-2, 19:1-10.

10. Jesus points out the inflated self-importance of the Jewish religious leaders in such verses as Matthew 23:5-7, Mark 12:38-40, Luke 11:43, 16:15, 18:9-14, 20:46; and John 9:39-41. This, as well as the leaders' hypocrisy and self-righteousness, led to friction between them and both Jesus and John the Baptist, which is evident in the following verses: Matthew 3:7-9, 5:20, 9:3, 9:11, 9:34, 12:2, 12:10-14, 12:22-24, 12:38-39, 15:1-2, 15:12, 16:1-4, 16:21, 17:3-9, 20:18-19, 21:15-16, 21:33-46, 22:15, 23:1-7, 23:13-33, 26:59, 26:65-66, 27:41-43, 27:62-63; Mark 2:6-7, 2:16, 2:24, 3:6, 3:22, 7:5, 8:11, 8:15, 8:31, 10:2-9, 10:32-34, 11:15-18, 11:27-33, 12:13-15, 14:1, 14:43, 14:55, 14:63-65, 15:31-32; Luke 5:20-21, 5:30, 5:33, 6:2, 6:6-11, 7:28-30, 7:36-49, 9:22, 11:37-54, 12:1, 15:1-2, 16:14-15, 19:37-40, 19:47, 20:1-26, 20:45-47, 22:2, 22:66-71, 23:10; John 7:31-32, 7:45-49, 8:3-6, 8:13, 9:13-16, 9:39-41, 11:47-53, 11:57, 12:42-43.

11. See, for example, Matthew 18:4, Philippians 4:5, and Proverbs 29:23. See also: Leviticus 16:29-31, 23:27-29, 23:32, 26:40-41; Numbers 29:7; Deuteronomy 8:2-3, 8:16; 2 Chronicles 7:14, 33:23, 36:12; Ezra 8:21; Psalms 10:17-18, 25:9, 37:11, 76:9; Proverbs 11:2, 15:33, 16:19, 18:12, 22:4; Isaiah 66:2; Micah 6:8; Zephaniah 2:3; Matthew 5:5, 23:12; Luke 1:51-52, 14:7-11, 18:9-14; 1 Corinthians 1:27-31; 13:4; Galatians 5:22-23, 6:1; Ephesians 4:1-2; Philippians 2:3; Colossians 3:12; 1 Timothy 3:2-3, 6:11; 2 Timothy 2:24-25; Titus 3:1-2; James 1:9-10, 1:21, 3:17-18, 4:6, 4:10; 1 Peter 2:18-19, 3:1, 3:4-5, 3:8-9, 3:15, 5:5-6

12. See for example: Exodus 10:3; Deuteronomy 8:14; 1 Samuel 2:3; 2 Kings 19:22; 2 Chronicles 33:23, 36:12; Job 33:17, 35:12, 40:11-12; Psalms 5:5, 10:2-4, 31:18, 36:11, 40:4, 59:12, 73:3-6, 75:4-5, 86:14, 94:2-4, 119:51, 119:69, 119:78, 119:85, 119:122, 123:4, 131:1, 140:5; Proverbs 8:13, 11:2, 14:16, 16:18-19, 18:12, 21:4, 21:24, 27:1-2, 28:25, 29:23, 30:12-13; Isaiah 37:23; Jeremiah 9:23, 43:2, 48:29-30; Dan 5:20-23; Hosea 5:5, 7:10; Obadiah

Ch. 3 – The Biggest Obstacle to Real Happiness

1:3; Habakkuk 2:4-5; Zephaniah 3:11; Malachi 3:13-15; Mark 7:22; Romans 1:30, 11:20; 1 Corinthians 3:21, 4:6-7, 4:18-19, 5:2, 5:6, 8:1-2, 13:4; 2 Corinthians 10:17-18, 12:20; Galatians 5:26; Ephesians 2:8-9; Philippians 2:3; 1 Timothy 3:6, 6:3-4, 6:17; 2 Timothy 3:2, 3:4; James 3:14, 4:6, 4:16; 1 Peter 5:5; 2 Peter 2:18; 1 John 2:16; Revelation 13:5.

Many verses warn that God will punish arrogant pride: Leviticus 23:29, 26:19; 1 Samuel 2:3-4; 2 Kings 19:28; 2 Chronicles 26:16-21, 32:25; Psalms 101:5, 119:21; Proverbs 15:25, 16:5; Isaiah 2:10-12, 2:17, 3:16-17, 5:15, 9:9-11, 10:12, 13:11, 16:6-7, 23:8-9, 25:10-12, 28:1-3, 37:29; Jeremiah 13:9, 13:15-17, 48:25-26, 49:16, 50:29-32; Ezekiel 7:10-12, 7:24, 16:49-50, 16:56-57, 24:21, 24:25, 30:6, 30:18-19, 32:12, 33:28; Daniel 4:37; Hosea 13:6-8; Amos 6:8; Zephaniah 2:8-11; Zechariah 9:6, 10:11; Malachi 4:1; Matthew 23:12; Luke 1:51-52.

13. Regarding Jesus' humility, see Matthew 11:29 and Philippians 2:8; see also Zechariah 9:9 (compare Matthew 21:4-5). Regarding Paul's humility, see Acts 20:19; 2 Corinthians 10:1; 1 Thessalonians 2:7.

14. 2 Samuel 6:21-22; see also 2 Samuel 12:13 and 12:16-17

15. 1 Kings 21:27-29

16. 2 Kings 22:18-20; 2 Chronicles 34:26-28

17. 2 Chronicles 12:5-8, 12:12

18. 2 Chronicles 32:26

19. 2 Chronicles 33:12-13

20. See, for example, Matthew 18:2-4 (we must humble ourselves like children); Mark 7:20-23 (pride defiles a man) and Luke 18:9-14 (the humble tax collector, rather than the conceited Pharisee, leaves the Temple justified)

21. See also, Matthew 23:12; Luke 1:52, 14:11, 18:14; 1 Peter 5:6.

Chapter 4
OUR FATHER

The Bible refers to God in many ways. He is of course the Creator,[1] but the Scriptures also describe him as a judge,[2] a king,[3] a shepherd,[4] and a friend.[5] The prophets Hosea, Jeremiah, and Ezekiel compare God to a husband with an unfaithful wife.[6] The most common name for God in the Old Testament is "Yahweh" (also spelled as "Jehovah"), which is used more than 6,000 times. This name is usually translated as "Lord."[7] But in the New Testament another name for God becomes prominent—Father.[8]

The New Testament writers often refer to God as the Father of Jesus Christ.[9] They also call him "Father"[10] or "the Father."[11] But more important for our purposes are the many New Testament references to God as *our* Father.[12] For example, Jesus says:

> "But I say to you, love your enemies and pray for those who persecute you, so that you may be sons of your Father who is in heaven."
> —Matthew 5:44-45

Of course, if God is our Father, then we must be his children, as John says:

> See how great a love the Father has bestowed on us, that we would be called children of God; and *such* we are. For this reason the world does not know us, because it did not know Him. Beloved, now we are children of God, and it has not appeared as yet what we will be.
> —1 John 3:1-2[13]

Similarly, Paul calls us God's *adopted* children.[14] God uses this analogy[15] of parent-child to illustrate his relationship with us because of the unique nature of the parent-child relationship, which is like no other in human society.

When we think of the qualities of a good parent, what comes to mind? Certainly, a good parent protects and provides for his children. And so does God.[16] A good parent teaches and disciplines her child. God does the same.[17] But most of all, a good parent loves her child unconditionally. Even when her child rebels against her authority, disobeys her, makes poor choices, and gets into trouble, that parent continues to love him, no matter what. God does, too.[18] And that is critical. In no other human relationship is love as completely unconditional as a parent's love for her child. God, who is perfect,[19] is also the perfect Parent. He radiates this unconditional love. One of Jesus' most famous parables illustrates this.

In the parable of the Prodigal Son,[20] a young man requests and receives his share of his father's wealth while the father is still alive. The young man then leaves home and wastes the money on immoral pleasures. Having run out of money, he begins to starve, and eventually decides to return home to seek forgiveness. But before the boy can even finish apologizing, his father has already pardoned him and begun to celebrate the son's homecoming. The father's behavior is a wonderful illustration of *agapaô*, the Greek word for selfless, self-giving, self-sacrificing love.[21] This is unconditional love that always sees value in the person loved. This is the love a good parent has for her child. And this is the love that God has for us.

Beyond Shallow Faith

When we view God as a loving parent, the New Testament comes into sharper focus. Unlike in other religions, God is not merely a judge, hunting for a reason to condemn us or impartially weighing our deeds on the scales of justice to see whether or not we deserve to go to Heaven.[22] He is instead a loving Father. We cannot earn his love through obedience or accomplishments or any manner of genuflection—because we already have it.

This is not to say that God approves of our bad behavior. Indeed, this is yet another parallel between our relationship with God and that of a child and her parent. As a child grows, her increasing desire for self-determination collides with her parents' efforts to instill proper values and to protect her from harmful choices. To the extent that she resists these efforts and insists on acting as she desires, she will alienate herself from her parents—a situation that often becomes most acute during the teenage years. Similarly, our selfish choices, inconsiderate conduct, and immorality estrange us from God.

Nevertheless, God continues to love us and remains eager to forgive us. We find forgiveness through repentance—that is, a change of heart.[23] Obedience—which is so fundamental in many religions—is secondary in Christianity, because God is far more interested in our hearts than in our behavior.

Our change of heart leads us back to God, to whom we surrender our very lives.[24] In doing so, we are obeying the greatest commandment:

> HEAR, O ISRAEL! THE LORD OUR GOD IS
> ONE LORD; AND YOU SHALL LOVE THE
> LORD YOUR GOD WITH ALL YOUR HEART,

AND WITH ALL YOUR SOUL, AND WITH
ALL YOUR MIND, AND WITH ALL YOUR
STRENGTH.

—Mark 12:29-30[25]

"Love" in this verse, as in most of the New Testament, is the Greek word, *agapaô*. As we have seen, this is the love that God has for us. This kind of love is not a feeling, but a choice. We "love" him by choosing to follow him, and by making him more important than anyone or anything else in our lives. In this way, we begin a loving relationship with him.

God's unconditional love for us also means that he is a God of second chances—and many more chances after that. Like the father in Jesus' parable of the Prodigal Son, God anxiously waits to reestablish the connection with each of us, as soon as we turn back to him. So no matter how bad we've been, or for how long, "our Father" stands ready to forgive his children. We simply need to come back to him.

Beyond Shallow Faith

Endnotes for Chapter Four, "Our Father"

1. See Genesis chapters 1-2. See also Ecclesiastes 12:1, Isaiah 27:11, 40:28, 43:1, 43:15; Romans 1:25; and 1 Peter 4:19.

2. See Genesis 18:25; Judges 11:27; Job 23:7; Psalms 7:11, 50:6, 75:7, 94:2; Isaiah 33:22; 2 Timothy 4:8; Hebrews 12:23; and James 5:9. Many other verses, too numerous to list, speak of God judging people. See, for example, 1 Samuel 2:10; 1 Chronicles 16:33; and Psalms 9:8, 67:4, 96:10.

3. See Psalms 5:2, 10:16, 24:7-10, 29:10, 44:4, 47:2, 47:6-7, 68:24, 84:3, 95:3, 98:6, 145:1, 149:2; Isaiah 6:5, 33:22, 41:21, 43:15, 44:6; Jeremiah 8:19, 10:7, 10:10, 46:18, 48:15, 51:57; Daniel 4:37; Zephaniah 3:15; Zechariah 14:9, 14:16-17; Malachi 1:14; Matthew 2:2, 25:34, 25:40; 1 Timothy 1:17, 6:15; Revelation 15:3, 17:14, 19:16. (And see Zechariah 9:9, Matthew 21:5, and John 12:15.)

4. See Genesis 49:24; Psalms 23:1, 28:9, 80:1; Isaiah 40:11; Jeremiah 31:10; Ezekiel 34:12; Matthew 26:31 (quoting Zechariah 13:7); Mark 14:27; John 10:11-14; Hebrews 13:20; 1 Peter 2:25, 5:4; Revelation 7:17.

5. See 2 Chronicles 20:7; Isaiah 41:8; Jeremiah 3:4; John 15:13-15.

6. The wife is, of course, the people of Israel and Judah, who were unfaithful to God. See Hosea 1:2, 2:2, 2:5-8, 2:10, 2:13; Jeremiah 3:1-2, 31:31-32; and Ezekiel 16:15-32. God is also compared to a husband in Isaiah 54:5-6, 2 Corinthians 11:2, and Revelation 21:2.

7. In Genesis alone, God is referred to as "Jehovah," or "Lord," in 148 different verses: Genesis 2:4-5, 2:7-9, 2:15-16, 2:18-19, 2:21-22, 3:1, 3:8-9, 3:13-14, 3:21-23, 4:1, 4:3-4, 4:6, 4:9, 4:13, 4:15-16, 4:26, 5:29, 6:3,. 6:5-8, 7:1, 7:5, 7:16, 8:20-21, 9:26, 10:9, 11:5-6, 11:8-9, 12:1, 12:4, 12:7-8, 12:17, 13:4, 13:10, 13:13-14, 13:18, 14:22, 15:1-2, 15:4, 15:6-8, 15:18, 16:2, 16:5, 16:7, 16:9-11, 16:13, 17:1, 18:1, 18:13-14, 18:17, 18:19-20, 18:22, 18:26-27, 18:30-33, 19:13-14, 19:16, 19:24, 19:27, 20:4, 20:18, 21:1, 21:33, 22:11, 22:14-16, 24:1, 24:3, 24:7, 24:12, 24:21, 24:26-27, 24:31, 24:35, 24:40, 24:42, 24:44, 24:48, 24:50-52, 24:56, 25:21-23, 26:2, 26:12, 26:22, 26:24-25, 26:28-29, 27:7, 27:20, 27:27, 28:13, 28:16, 28:21, 29:31-33, 29:35, 30:24, 30:27, 30:30, 31:3, 31:49, 32:9, 38:7, 38:10, 39:2-3, 39:5, 39:21, 39:23, 49:18.

8. Only one book of the New Testament—the very short 3rd letter of John—fails to refer to God as Father. God is also sometimes represented

as a Father in the Old Testament. See, for example: Deuteronomy 32:6; Psalms 68:5; Isaiah 9:6, 63:16, 64:8; Jeremiah 3:4, 3:19, 31:9.

9. See Matthew 7:21, 10:32-33, 11:25-27, 12:50, 15:13, 16:17, 16:27, 18:10, 18:19, 18:35, 20:23, 25:31-34, 26:39, 26:42, 26:53; Mark 8:38; Luke 10:21-22, 22:28-30, 24:49; John 5:17, 5:18, 6:32, 6:40, 8:19, 8:38, 8:49, 8:54, 10:18, 10:29-30, 10:37, 14:7, 14:20-21, 14:23, 15:1, 15:8, 15:15, 15:23-24, 20:17; Romans 15:6; 2 Corinthians 1:3, 11:31, Ephesians 1:3; Colossians 1:3; 1 Peter 1:3; 2 Peter 1:17; 1 John 1:3, 2:22-24, 4:14; 2 John 1:3, 1:9; Revelation 1:6, 2:27, 3:5, 3:21, 14:1.

10. See Mark 14:36; Luke 22:41-42, 23:34, 23:46; John 8:41-42, 11:41, 12:28, 17:1, 17:5, 17:11, 17:21, 17:24-25; Ephesians 4:6; Hebrews 1:5, 2:11.

11. See Matthew 24:36, 28:19; Mark 13:32; Luke 9:26; John 1:14, 1:18, 3:35, 4:21-23, 5:19-23, 5:26, 5:36-37, 5:45, 6:27, 6:37, 6:44-46, 6:57, 6:65, 8:16, 8:18, 8:27-28, 10:15, 10:17, 10:32, 10:36, 10:38, 12:26, 12:49-50, 13:1, 13:3, 14:6, 14:8-13, 14:16, 14:26, 14:28, 14:31, 15:9, 15:16, 15:26, 16:3, 16:10, 16:15, 16:17, 16:23, 16:25-28, 16:32, 18:11, 20:21; Acts 1:4, 1:7, 2:33; Romans 6:4; 1 Corinthians 8:6, 15:24; Galatians 1:1; Ephesians 1:17, 2:18, 3:14, 5:20, 6:23; Philippians 2:11; Colossians 1:12, 3:17; 1 Thessalonians 1:1; 2 Thessalonians 1:2; 1 Timothy 1:2; 2 Timothy 1:2; Titus 1:4; James 1:17; 1 Peter 1:2; 1 John 1:2, 2:1, 2:13, 2:15-16; 2 John 1:4; Jude 1:1.

12. See Matthew 5:16, 5:44-45, 5:48, 6:1, 6:3-4, 6:6, 6:8, 6:9, 6:14-15, 6:17-18, 6:26, 6:32, 7:11, 10:20, 10:29, 13:43, 18:14, 23:9; Mark 11:25-26; Luke 6:36, 11:13, 12:30, 12:32; Romans 1:7; 1 Corinthians 1:3; 2 Corinthians 1:2, 6:18; Galatians 1:3-4; Ephesians 1:2; Philippians 1:2, 4:20; Colossians 1:2; 1 Thessalonians 1:3, 3:11, 3:13; 2 Thessalonians 1:1, 2:16; Philemon 1:3; James 1:27, 3:9.

13. See also John 1:12, 11:52; Acts 17:28-29; Romans 8:15-17, 8:21, 9:8; 2 Corinthians 6:18; Galatians 4:4-7; Philippians 2:15; Hebrews 12:7-10; 1 Peter 1:14; 1 John 3:10, 5:1, 5:2.

14. Romans 8:15-17

15. Whether you believe that the New Testament writings were penned by God through the hand of men, or by men under God's inspiration, or were simply written by men with a deep understanding of God and His ways, I believe the result is the same: God was the ultimate source of those writings.

16. See Genesis 1:29-30, 9:2-3; Exodus 16:2-18, 16:35, 17:1-6, 23:20; Numbers 11:4-6, 11:31-32, 20:2-11; Deuteronomy 8:7-10; Ruth 1:6; 1 Kings 17:2-16; Job 36:31; Psalms 12:5-7, 32:7, 36:6-7, 40:11, 61:2-4, 78:24-29, 91:11, 104:10-15, 104:27-28, 121:2-8; Isaiah 52:12; Daniel 12:1.

17. See Hebrews 12:4-11. See also, Deuteronomy 4:36, 8:5, 11:2; Proverbs 3:11-12; Revelation 3:19.

18. See, for example, Romans 5:6-8.

19. See Matthew 5:48.

20. Luke 15:11-32

21. When you see the English word "love" in the New Testament, the original Greek is always either *agapaô* (or a derivation thereof) or *phileô* (or a derivation thereof). The latter refers to brotherly love (as in Philadelphia, "City of Brotherly Love"). *Agapaô* is used in about six times as many New Testament verses as *phileô*. For more on this, see Chapter Ten, "Is Free Will an Illusion?"

22. For example, the Koran says: "We shall set up just scales on the Day of Resurrection, so that no man shall in the least be wronged. Actions as small as a grain of mustard seed shall be weighed out. Our reckoning shall suffice." (21:47) Also: "Those whose good deeds weigh heavy in the scales shall triumph, but those whose deeds are light shall forfeit their souls and abide in Hell forever." (23:102-103) See also, 18:49, 34:3-5, 69:18, 82:9-16. (The quotations in this footnote are from Dawood, *The Koran*.)

23. The Greek word which is translated "repent" is *metanoeô*, which means "to change one's mind or purpose." In short, repentance means to turn back to God. The New Testament teaches that repentance is the starting point for reconciliation with God. See Matthew 3:2, 4:17; Mark 1:4, 1:15, 6:12; Luke 3:3, 5:32, 13:3, 13:5, 15:7, 24:47; Acts 2:38, 3:19, 8:22, 13:24, 17:30, 19:4, 20:21, 26:20; 2 Corinthians 7:9-10; 2 Timothy 2:25; 2 Peter 3:9; Revelation 2:5, 2:16, 2:21-22, 3:3, 3:19, 9:20-21, 16:9, 16:11.

24. When the New Testament talks of "faith" and "belief," the Greek word is *pistis*, or its verb form, *pisteuô*, both of which imply trust, commitment, or surrender. For more on this, see Chapter Ten, "Is Free Will an Illusion?"

25. See also Matthew 22:36-38. The words in all capitals are quoting Deuteronomy 6:4-5. See also Deuteronomy 13:3 and 30:6.

Chapter 5
REBELLION AND REPENTANCE

Adam blew it for all of us.[1] So says Paul, the first century Christian missionary and author of thirteen letters in the New Testament.[2] Through Adam, sin and death entered the world and spread to each one of us.[3] Even though we did not personally commit the "offense of Adam" (Romans 5:14),[4] his transgression brought God's condemnation on all of us. We are all transgressors like him.[5] Of course, Eve also did her part, as Paul points out in 1 Timothy 2:14.[6]

Did these terrible consequences flow from merely eating fruit?[7] Since the forbidden fruit was "the knowledge of good and evil" (Genesis 2:9 and 2:17), was God trying to keep Adam and Eve ignorant? Or was this really about Adam and Eve having sex,[8] as some followers of Sun Myung Moon[9] told me when I was in college? No, no, and no.

The problem went far deeper than these superficial explanations. When Adam and Eve ate the fruit, they were rebelling against God. And as a result of their rebellion, God expelled them from the Garden of Eden.

But perhaps it could have been different. When I read the stories of King Saul and King David, I believe the story of Adam and Eve could have turned out better despite their disobedience. However, let's begin with their rebellion.

God told Adam not to eat from the tree of the knowledge of good and evil:

> The Lord God commanded the man, saying, "From any tree of the garden you may eat freely; but from the tree of the knowledge of good

and evil you shall not eat, for in the day that
you eat from it you will surely die."

—Genesis 2:16-17

Adam and Eve both disobeyed God by eating the tree's
fruit.[10] But the couple's mere disobedience is not as significant as the *reason* they disobeyed him. Let's take a closer
look at how the serpent tricked Eve.[11]

The Temptation. The serpent begins by asking her a
simple question: "Indeed, has God said, 'You shall not eat
from any tree of the garden?' " (Genesis 3:1) This is a strange
question with which to begin a conversation. So Eve and the
serpent must have been talking for awhile, and the serpent
was constantly probing for weakness. He finds it here, for
Eve makes a critical mistake in her response:

> The woman said to the serpent, "From the fruit
> of the trees of the garden we may eat; but from
> the fruit of the tree which is in the middle of
> the garden, God has said, 'You shall not eat
> from it or touch it, or you will die.' "
>
> —Genesis 3:2-3

God never said they couldn't *touch* the fruit, but Eve
apparently misremembered or misunderstood.[12] And I'm
convinced the serpent used that mistake to undermine Eve's
trust in God, for the crafty snake immediately responds,
"You surely will not die!" (Genesis 3:4)

In my imagination I see the serpent touching the fruit
to prove his point, and Eve being shocked when he doesn't
die! What thoughts must have gone through her mind at
that point? *Was God wrong? Did he lie?* And then the serpent
seizes the initiative:

> For God knows that in the day you eat from it
> your eyes will be opened, and you will be like
> God, knowing good and evil.
>
> —Genesis 3:5

The most effective lie always contains an element of truth, and so it is here. Part of what the serpent says is true: "your eyes will be opened . . . knowing good and evil." That in fact happened: "Then the eyes of both of them [Adam and Eve] were opened, and they knew that they were naked." (Genesis 3:7) The lie was what the cunning serpent cleverly sandwiched in between: "and you will be like God."

Eve found the temptation to "be like God" difficult to resist. She was undoubtedly attracted by the idea that she would not have to follow God's rules anymore. She could decide for herself. She would be in control. The snake appealed to her arrogance, to her desire to be self-sufficient and independent—to that fatal flaw in human beings that we call pride. In short, she was tempted by the idea that she wouldn't need God anymore. And this was the crux of the problem. Eve wasn't just disobeying God—she was rejecting him.

Now we must be clear about this. Eve was not rejecting God in the sense that she did not love him or want to be near him, but she was rejecting his dominion over her. This was nothing less than a rebellion. She wanted to "be like God" in that she wanted the freedom to do as she pleased instead of following his rules. She was like the sixteen-year-old who wants to stay out late and go wherever she wants, with whomever she pleases, instead of obeying her parents.

This desire to "be like God" is a universal human flaw. It means we want to be in charge. We want to make our own rules. We want to decide for ourselves what is right and wrong. We may be fine with God's rules up to a point, but not when they get in the way of what we really want to do.

For example, we may agree that adultery is morally wrong, especially when we are the victim of it.[13] But if our heart—or our lust—leads us into an adulterous relationship that is fun and fulfilling, then many of us are willing to disregard that rule in our own situation. Similarly, if our marriage isn't working out to our satisfaction, we may decide that divorce is actually acceptable, even though God hates divorce.[14] And of course, we all tend to condemn others in our hearts and in our speech, even though Jesus told us not to judge others.[15] Unfortunately, when we reject God's dominion, we are rebelling against him just as Eve did.

The Clincher. Of course, the serpent not only provided the motive for Eve to break God's rule—"you will be like God"—but also shrewdly nullified the threatened consequence: "You surely will not die!" He exploits the ambiguity in what God had said. The term, "die," could have at least three potential meanings: (1) immediate physical death, (2) future physical death, or (3) spiritual death. In hindsight, God must have meant either (2) or (3), or both, but the snake adopts the first meaning, and Eve doesn't question this.

Removing the adverse consequences of our rule-breaking greatly increases the likelihood of giving in to the temptation, sometimes to the point that rule-breaking becomes virtually inevitable. The examples of this principle are almost endless. How many of us jaywalk or drive a little over the speed limit because the police don't bother enforcing such slight violations? How many of us have taken a few office supplies from work because no one would miss them? Eve ate the forbidden fruit in part because of the temptation to "be like God," but also because she believed the serpent's lie that there would be no adverse consequences for her disobedience. Similarly, Adam ate after seeing that Eve had eaten and suffered no apparent ill effects.

The Hammer Falls. However, even after Adam and Eve disobeyed God, all may not have been lost. The Lord does not seem upset at first:

> Then the Lord God called to the man, and said to him, "Where are you?" He said, "I heard the sound of You in the garden, and I was afraid because I was naked; so I hid myself." And He said, "Who told you that you were naked? Have you eaten from the tree of which I commanded you not to eat?"
>
> —Genesis 3:9-11

Some have argued that God's remarks contradict the idea that he is omniscient. Why did he ask Adam if he had eaten the forbidden fruit? Didn't he already know what Adam and Eve had done? Certainly he did. But I don't believe he could be certain about how they would react when he confronted them about their disobedience.[16] So instead of immediately pronouncing judgment, God gave them a chance to repent. Regrettably, their subsequent behavior sealed their doom. Instead of confessing and throwing themselves on the mercy of God, they made excuses and blamed others:

> The man said, "The woman whom You gave *to be* with me, she gave me from the tree, and I

ate." Then the Lord God said to the woman, "What is this you have done?" And the woman said, "The serpent deceived me, and I ate."

—Genesis 3:12-13

At that point, the hammer fell. God decreed that the woman would have to suffer the pains of childbirth,[17] while the man would have to labor hard to obtain food for himself and his family.[18] And of course, both were forced to leave the beautiful, bountiful Garden of Eden.[19]

Saul and David. I believe it could have been much different for Adam and Eve when I see the disparate treatment of Saul and David after each suffered moments of weakness.

David, as king of Israel, committed adultery with Bathsheba, the wife of Uriah the Hittite. When she became pregnant, David arranged for Uriah to die in battle in order to cover up the misdeed, after which David took Bathsheba as his own wife.[20]

King Saul's offenses were twofold: (1) he offered sacrifices to God without authority to do so, rather than waiting for Samuel's overdue arrival at a battlefield,[21] and (2) he took booty from the Amalekites, and took their king prisoner, after God told him to destroy them and all that they possessed.[22]

To me, David's offenses seem much more egregious than Saul's. Yet God punished Saul by passing the throne of Israel to David, rather than to any of Saul's sons.[23] David, on the other hand, was able to leave his crown to his descendants.[24]

Beyond Shallow Faith

Why did the Lord treat Saul more harshly than David? The answer lies—at least in part—in their reactions when confronted with their wrongdoing.

When Samuel finally arrived at the battlefield and asked Saul why he had made sacrifices to God without authority, he replied:

> Because I saw that the people were scattering from me, and that you did not come within the appointed days, and that the Philistines were assembling at Michmash, therefore I said, "Now the Philistines will come down against me at Gilgal, and I have not asked the favor of the Lord." So I forced myself and offered the burnt offering.
>
> —1 Samuel 13:11-12

Saul blamed the people, Samuel, and even the Philistines—everyone but himself. Similarly, he placed responsibility on the Israelites for failing to carry out the Lord's command to destroy the Amalekites:

> They [the people] have brought them [livestock] from the Amalekites, for the people spared the best of the sheep and oxen, to sacrifice to the Lord your God; but the rest we have utterly destroyed.
>
> —1 Samuel 15:15

Like Saul, Adam and Eve blamed others for their misbehavior. Adam blamed Eve and even, by implication, God ("The woman whom You gave *to be* with me"). Eve of course blamed the serpent ("The serpent deceived me").

Now contrast this with David's reaction when Nathan the prophet exposed his wrongdoing and pronounced God's judgment on him: "I have sinned against the Lord." (2 Samuel 12:13) David's response was remarkable in its starkness and humility. This powerful and popular king — who could easily have had Nathan executed or imprisoned — made no excuses and blamed no one else. David just admitted that he messed up. Simply put, he repented. And God was merciful. Perhaps Adam and Eve would also have found God to be merciful if they had admitted their wrongdoing and repented. To be sure, they would have been punished, as David was,[25] but maybe they could have remained in Eden.

The Lesson For Us. There is a lesson here for us. If we humbly admit that we have done wrong, and repent — that is, turn back to God and his ways — then we too will find a merciful God who is eager to forgive us. And unlike Adam and Eve, we know we can expect a favorable reception from God if we do so:

> But God demonstrates His own love toward us, in that while we were yet sinners, Christ died for us. Much more then, having now been justified by His blood, we shall be saved from the wrath *of God* through Him. For if while we were enemies we were reconciled to God through the death of His Son, much more, having been reconciled, we shall be saved by His life.
>
> —Romans 5:8-9

In Jesus' parable of the prodigal son,[26] the younger of two sons receives his inheritance while his father is still alive. That son then leaves home and squanders all of his money on wicked living. But when he realizes his mistake and returns home, he does not receive the condemnation he expects. Instead, his father runs to embrace him. We are that younger son, and God is the father. When we return to God, he runs to embrace us.[27]

There's just one catch—we have to return.[28] I don't mean to imply that we must become perfect, since none of us will achieve perfection in this life. But we must repent. That is, we need to have a *change of heart*. We must surrender to God and accept his dominion over our lives. We need to stop trying to make our own rules and start trying to live by God's rules, trusting that he knows what is best for us. We have to end our rebellion.

And to truly accomplish this, we must do what Adam, Eve, and Saul failed to do—admit we have done wrong, without excuses and without blaming anyone else. As we have seen, that is what King David did, and that is also what the younger son in Jesus' parable did, after he "came to his senses" (Luke 15:17):

> I will get up and go to my father and will say to him, "Father, I have sinned against heaven, and in your sight; I am no longer worthy to be called your son; make me as one of your hired men."
>
> —Luke 15:18-19

When the young man in the parable repented and returned, he was not in fact treated as a hired hand by his father, but as a loved and treasured son.[29] After King David repented, he and his descendants remained as kings over Judah for four centuries,[30] and one of his descendants became the earthly father of Jesus,[31] the "King of Kings." (1 Timothy 6:15)[32] Both David and the younger son received mercy because of their humble repentance. And so will we.

Beyond Shallow Faith

Endnotes for Chapter Five, "Rebellion and Repentance"

1. I am not concerned with whether the story of Adam and Eve is literal truth, allegory, parable, or something else. The characters are true to life and the lessons the story teaches are worthwhile regardless of how it is interpreted.

2. Paul wrote the following thirteen letters: Romans, 1 Corinthians, 2 Corinthians, Galatians, Ephesians, Philippians, Colossians, 1 Thessalonians, 2 Thessalonians, 1 Timothy, 2 Timothy, Titus, and Philemon

3. See, for example, Romans 5:12, 5:15, and 5:17, and 1 Corinthians 15:22.

4. Romans 5:14 says, in relevant part: "Nevertheless death reigned . . . even over those who had not sinned in the likeness of the offense of Adam."

5. See Romans 5:18-19.

6. 1 Timothy 2:14: "And *it was* not Adam *who* was deceived, but the woman being deceived, fell into transgression."

7. Although the fruit eaten by Adam and Eve has traditionally been viewed as an apple, Genesis merely refers to it as "fruit." See, for example, Genesis 3:2-3 and 3:6.

8. While this is perhaps an interesting idea, I find no support for it in Genesis—especially since the author of Genesis explicitly talks about Adam and Eve having sex, and Eve becoming pregnant, in chapter four. See Genesis 4:1 and 4:25.

9. Moon (1920-2012) founded the Unification Church in South Korea. He died on September 3, 2012.

10. See Genesis 3:6.

11. The serpent is traditionally associated with Satan, although Genesis does not explicitly say that.

12. In fairness to Eve, she was not even created when God first announced the commandment, so perhaps she only learned about it from Adam. See Genesis 2:16-23.

13. The prohibition against adultery is one of the Ten Commandments. See Exodus 20:14 and Deuteronomy 5:18. In the Old Testament, adultery was punishable by death. See Leviticus 20:10. The New Testament also

condemns adultery. See, for example, Matthew 5:27-28, 5:32, 19:9, 19:16-19; Mark 10:11-12, 10:17-19; Luke 16:18, 18:18-20; Romans 13:9; Galatians 5:19; 2 Peter 2:14. Even in the case of the woman caught in adultery, Jesus does not approve of her behavior, but tells her, "Go and sin no more." (See John 8:3-11, which are actually not found in the oldest manuscripts of John's gospel.)

14. Malachi 2:16 says that God hates divorce. See also Malachi 2:13-15; Matthew 19:3-9; Mark 10:2-12; and 1 Corinthians 7:11. The only ground for divorce that Jesus recognized was unfaithfulness—i.e., adultery. See Matthew 19:9.

15. See Matthew 7:1, Luke 6:37, Romans 14:13, and James 4:11.

16. I say this because I believe God has given people free will, and because I believe that a person's free choices are to some degree unpredictable and unforeseeable, even for God.

17. Genesis 3:16

18. Genesis 3:17-19

19. Genesis 3:23-24

20. See 2 Samuel 11:1-26.

21. See 1 Samuel 10:8 and 13:1-12.

22. See 1 Samuel 15:1-9.

23. See 1 Samuel 13:13-14, 15:10-29, 28:17-18, and 31:1-7. Although 1 Samuel 28:17-18 says that God took the kingdom from Saul because of his failure to destroy the Amalekites, it seems clear from 1 Samuel 13:13-14 that God had already formed this intention based on the earlier offense.

24. See, for example, 2 Samuel 7:12-16; 1 Kings 1:28-40, 2:4

25. First of all, the child conceived through David and Bethsheba's adultery died. See 2 Samuel 12:15-18. But that was not all, for the Lord told David, "I will raise up evil against you from your own household; I will even take your wives before your eyes and give them to your companion, and he will lie with your wives in broad daylight." (2 Samuel 12:11) Subsequent events fulfilled this prophecy. David's son Amnon raped Tamar, the sister of Absalom, who was another of David's sons. (2 Samuel 13:1-22) Then Absalom had Amnon killed in retaliation.

(2 Samuel 13:23-33) Thereafter, Absalom led a revolt against his father, David, and captured Jerusalem, where Absalom slept with David's concubines. (2 Samuel 15:1-12, 16:15-22) Absalom's revolt ended when he was defeated and slain. (2 Samuel 18:1-14)

26. Luke 15:11-32

27. See Luke 15:20.

28. Note that the father in Jesus' parable does not go after his wayward son, but remains at home and awaits the boy's return. See Luke 15:13-20.

29. See Luke 15:22-24.

30. David's descendants ruled the kingdom of Judah until King Zedekiah was carried into captivity by the Babylonians in 586 B.C. Per 1st and 2nd Kings, 1st and 2nd Chronicles, and Jeremiah, those kings were, in order: Solomon, Rehoboam, Abijah (a/k/a Abijam or Abia), Asa, Jehoshaphat, Jehoram (a/k/a Joram), Ahaziah (a/k/a Jehoahaz), Joash (a/k/a Jehoash), Amaziah, Azariah (a/k/a Uzziah), Jotham, Ahaz, Hezekiah, Manasseh, Amon, Josiah, Jehoahaz (a/k/a : Joahaz or Shallum), Jehoiakim (a/k/a Eliakim), Jehoiachin (a/k/a Coniah or Jeconiah), and Zedekiah.

31. See Matthew 1:1-16 and Luke 3:23-31.

32. See also Revelation 17:14 and 19:16.

Chapter 6
FAITH AND WORKS

What did James have in mind when he said "faith, if it has no works, is dead" (James 2:17) and "faith without works is useless" (James 2:20)? Did he really mean that faith without works cannot save, as he implies in James 2:14?:

> What use is it, my brethren, if someone says he
> has faith but he has no works? Can that faith
> save him?

When James said, "You see that a man is justified by works and not by faith alone" (James 2:24), was he contradicting Paul, who said, "by the works of the Law no flesh will be justified in His sight" (Romans 3:20) and "a man is not justified by the works of the Law but through faith in Christ Jesus" (Galatians 2:16)?

Actually, James and Paul do not disagree, but to see this clearly we must view these verses in context.

As Paul says in Romans 3:20 and Galatians 2:16, he is talking about "works of the Law"—that is, the Jewish effort to please God by obeying the Jewish Law, as contained in the first five books of the Bible.[1] These "works of the Law" include, among other things, offering the required animal sacrifices, obeying the Ten Commandments and other laws, and circumcising all males.

The Jews had repeatedly failed in their attempts to scrupulously observe the Jewish Law, as Peter recognized when he admitted that the Law was a "yoke which neither our fathers nor we have been able to bear." (Acts 15:10) Therefore, the early Christians quickly concluded that Gentile converts to Christianity need not comply with the requirements of the Jewish Law.[2] Indeed, Paul went further and warned the Galatians not to even try to follow the Law, because: "You have been severed from Christ, you who are seeking to be justified by law; you have fallen from grace." (Galatians 5:4)

For Paul, the only way to be justified—that is, to be made just and righteous in God's sight, and thus be saved— is through faith in Jesus Christ: "For we maintain that a man is justified by faith apart from works of the Law." (Romans 3:28) Because of our faith, God saves us through his grace (unmerited favor): "For by grace you have been saved through faith; and that not of yourselves, *it is* the gift of God; not as a result of works, so that no one may boast." (Ephesians 2:8-9) And what does this faith involve? Paul tells us:

> But what does it say? "THE WORD IS NEAR YOU, IN YOUR MOUTH AND IN YOUR HEART"—that is, the word of faith which we are preaching, that if you confess with your mouth Jesus *as* Lord, and believe in your heart that God raised Him from the dead, you will be saved; for with the heart a person believes, resulting in righteousness, and with the mouth he confesses, resulting in salvation.
>
> —Romans 10:8-10[3]

For Paul, faith requires more than mere intellectual assent to certain biblical truths. We must sincerely believe in Christ's resurrection, which is the cornerstone of Christianity and the ultimate proof of Jesus' claims of divine status. Therefore, when we believe in our hearts that Christ was raised from the dead, we acknowledge him as God. Then we must act on that belief through an honest confession that Jesus is Lord—not merely *a* lord, mind you, but *our* Lord. In doing so, we surrender ourselves to Christ and submit to his Lordship over our lives.

Now let's look at what James means by "works." He gives us two examples from the Old Testament. First, there's Abraham:

> Was not Abraham our father justified by works when he offered up Isaac his son on the altar? You see that faith was working with his works, and as a result of the works, faith was perfected; and the Scripture was fulfilled which says, "AND ABRAHAM BELIEVED GOD, AND IT WAS RECKONED TO HIM AS RIGHTEOUSNESS," and he was called the friend of God. You see that a man is justified by works and not by faith alone.
>
> —James 2:21-24[4]

What James calls Abraham's "works" had nothing to do with law or righteous behavior or a kindness extended to strangers. Abraham's "works" were simply an act of obedience. God told him to sacrifice his son Isaac, and Abraham obeyed—until an angel stopped him at the last moment.[5]

The other example James uses to illustrate "works" is Rahab the harlot, who hid the Israelite spies from the authorities in Jericho and then helped the spies escape, all because of her faith in the Lord:[6]

> In the same way, was not Rahab the harlot also justified by works when she received the messengers and sent them out by another way? For

just as the body without *the* spirit is dead, so
also faith without works is dead.

—James 2:25-26

As with Abraham, Rahab's "works" did not involve
righteous behavior—she was a prostitute, after all. And
while she showed kindness to the two Israelite spies by hiding them and helping them escape, this wasn't exactly an act
of charity. She believed the Lord would help the Israelites
destroy Jericho, and she wanted to save herself and her family from the coming devastation. Nevertheless, she acted in
faith by hiding the spies, at great risk to her own safety.

So we see that by "works" James just means faith *in
action*. As with Paul, this kind of faith goes beyond mere belief. Such faith does not simply *wish* that the poor would be
helped, but *acts* to help them in tangible ways:

If a brother or sister is without clothing and in
need of daily food, and one of you says to
them, "Go in peace, be warmed and be filled,"
and yet you do not give them what is necessary for *their* body, what use is that? Even so
faith, if it has no works, is dead, *being* by itself.

—James 2:15-17

Bungee-jumping is a terrifying experience for those of
us who have a fear of falling. I can *say* that I have faith in
those elastic cords that I hope will save me from certain
death, but the proof of my faith is when I actually jump. Similarly, I may agree that flying is the safest form of travel,
but if I refuse to get on an airplane for fear of crashing my
agreement is just words. When I get in my car to drive
somewhere, I am putting into action my faith that the other

drivers on the road will obey the traffic laws that keep us all safe, such as stopping at red lights and driving on the right-hand side of the road. In each instance, James would say my faith is dead unless and until I *act* on it by jumping, flying, or driving.

Of course, Christianity is not about having faith in elastic cords, airplanes, or other drivers, but about faith in Jesus Christ. But the principle is the same. I can say that I have faith in Jesus Christ, but if that faith never translates into action—if it never affects the way I live—then James and Paul would agree that I lack genuine, sincere faith.

Real faith requires action, such as: praying, reading God's Word, and trying to obey the two greatest commandments: (1) "love the Lord your God with all your heart, and with all your soul, and with all your mind, and with all your strength" (Mark 12:30),[7] and (2) "love your neighbor as yourself" (Matthew 22:39).[8] We obey those two greatest commandments, for example, when we worship God, give back to God, give to the poor, and serve others.

Faith in action will gradually result in spiritual growth, spiritual maturity, and, yes, good works. In other words, faith in action leads to more Christ-like behavior. But to be clear, good works and Christ-like behavior are not the *cause* of our salvation, but the *result* of it. We are saved by God's grace. He gives us salvation, which we do not deserve, because of our faith in Jesus Christ. James and Paul would agree on that, too.

Beyond Shallow Faith

Endnotes for Chapter Six, "Faith and Works"

1. The first five books of the Bible are: Genesis, Exodus, Leviticus, Numbers, and Deuteronomy.

2. See Acts 15:1-29.

3. The quotation is from Deuteronomy 30:14.

4. The quotation is from Genesis 15:6.

5. See Genesis 22:1-14.

6. See Joshua 2:1-21.

7. See also Matthew 22:37, Luke 10:27, and Deuteronomy 6:5.

8. See also Matthew 19:19, Mark 12:31, Luke 10:27, Romans 13:9, Galatians 5:14, James 2:8, and Leviticus 19:18.

Chapter 7
THREE LIES PEOPLE TELL ABOUT SATAN

In chapter six of my previous book,[1] I pointed out that people lie to us all the time. Some lies are little white lies or half-truths, while others are utter falsehoods. Often people lie to save our feelings. Sometimes they lie because they want something from us, such as our money or our favor. But I believe when people lie about Satan, they usually do so out of ignorance.[2] Let's look at three common falsehoods associated with Satan.

Lie #1: Satan doesn't exist. Satan goes by many names in the Bible. Most writers call him Satan or the devil,[3] but he is also known as Beelzebul[4] and in Revelation, he is a dragon.[5] Yet the Bible seems very clear on this point—Satan *does* exist. All four Gospel writers mention him, as does Paul, James, Peter, Jude, and the writer of Hebrews.[6] In the Old Testament, the writers of 1 Chronicles, Job, and Zechariah each refer to Satan.[7] If you believe the Bible, then someone or something that goes by the name of Satan must exist.

Lie #2: Satan can make you do something you don't want to do. Geraldine Jones, a character created by the late comedian Flip Wilson,[8] had a ready excuse for every misdeed: "The devil made me do it." Fortunately, Satan cannot truly *make* us do anything. Unfortunately, he doesn't need to.

Make no mistake, Satan has great power—for example, the Bible tells us that he has the power to cause sickness,[9] to oppress people,[10] to torment people,[11] and to hinder our plans.[12] He claimed to have dominion over all of the kingdoms of the world, since he offered them to Jesus.[13]

With God's permission, Satan was able to deprive Job of his possessions, his children, and his health.[14] Satan can even plant wicked ideas in our heads, as he did with King David, Judas Iscariot, Ananias, and probably Peter.[15] Yet the Bible never says that Satan can force us do something against our will—as God *can*, by the way.[16] So Satan uses other methods to lead us astray.

One of these methods is through lies and deception. We saw an example of this in Chapter Five, in the Garden of Eden, when the serpent—almost certainly symbolic of Satan—tells Eve that if she eats the forbidden fruit, "you will be like God, knowing good and evil." (Genesis 3:5) Enticed by this lie, Eve ate the fruit, and then learned to her dismay that she was not truly "like God." Satan had deceived her. She believed the lie and suffered the consequences.

Jesus calls Satan "a liar and the father of lies." (John 8:44) In the last days, Satan will use signs and false miracles to deceive many people.[17] Yet this is not the only arrow in Satan's quiver—and perhaps not even the most powerful one, for another weapon is often more useful and far more destructive: temptation.

Lies and deception trick us into doing wrong; temptation preys on our *desire* to do wrong. Satan unsuccessfully tempted Jesus in the wilderness.[18] Paul says Satan can tempt married couples if they withhold sexual relations from each other for very long.[19] The Lord's Prayer speaks of temptation in the same breath with "deliver us from evil" (Matthew 6:13)—or in some translations, "from the evil one."[20] Since James tells us that God "does not tempt anyone" (James 1:13), the Lord's Prayer seems to be asking God to keep Satan from tempting us. This request is similar to Jesus' advice to his disciples, "Pray that you may not enter into temptation." (Luke 22:40)

Giving in to temptation opens the door to Satan, for when we allow ourselves to sin, we give the devil an opportunity to undermine our commitment to God.[21] Paul speaks of the devil ensnaring us if we are not careful.[22] Nevertheless, giving in to temptation, or resisting it, remains *our* choice, not Satan's. He does not have power over us unless we give it to him, and with God's help we can resist Satan.[23] As Paul says in 1 Corinthians 10:13:

> No temptation has overtaken you but such as is common to man; and God is faithful, who will not allow you to be tempted beyond what you are able, but with the temptation will provide the way of escape also, so that you will be able to endure it.

When we give in to temptation, the devil didn't make us do it.

Lie #3: Satan's ways are more fun than God's ways. So why do people so often give in to temptation? I believe the answer is obvious: they think it will be more fun or more pleasurable than obeying God. But this too is a lie, and it is without doubt the most destructive lie of the three, not only because of its devastating impact on our earthly lives, but also because of its potential eternal consequences.

Before we go further, let's be clear about the differences between Satan's ways and God's ways. The Bible tells us a lot about the latter, but perhaps it largely boils down to one word: love. God tells us to love him with all our heart, mind, soul, and strength,[24] to love other Christians,[25] and to love our "neighbor" (Matthew 22:39),[26] which Jesus seems to define as anyone in need of our love.[27] As I pointed out in Chapter Four ("Our Father"), this kind of love is not an emotion, but a choice. When we choose to love in this way, we build a relationship with God through Jesus Christ. That relationship cultivates Paul's "fruit of the Spirit": "love, joy, peace, patience, kindness, goodness, faithfulness, gentleness, self-control." (Galatians 5:22-23) Paul's "fruit of the Spirit" is a pretty good summary of God's ways.

On the other hand, Satan's ways include such things as murder,[28] prolonged anger,[29] deceit and fraud,[30] immorality and idolatry,[31] and false righteousness.[32] According to Luke, Satan and his followers are enemies of righteousness, and prefer the darkness of evil over the light of God's ways.[33] The follower of Satan practices sin[34] and takes pleasure in wickedness.[35] Thus, the follower of Satan is entangled by the "deeds of the flesh," such as "immorality, impurity, sensuality, idolatry, sorcery, enmities, strife, jealousy, outbursts of anger, disputes, dissensions, factions, envying, drunkenness, carousing, and things like these." (Galatians 5:19-21)

Embracing wickedness makes a relationship with God impossible, for he cannot or will not unite Himself with evil. That is why Christ had to come and die, in order to restore the possibility of a connection between God and those willing to repent and surrender themselves to him.

Now back to our question of why people choose Satan's ways over God's ways—i.e., because they believe the former will be more enjoyable. And they are usually right, *but only for a time.* Sin is often pleasant in the short term, until the consequences begin to manifest themselves. This is what the author of Hebrews calls "the passing pleasures of sin." (Hebrews 11:25)

Adultery may be fun—until it loses its novelty or breaks up your marriage. Promiscuous sex might be exciting at first, but not after you end up with a sexually transmitted disease, an unwanted child, or perhaps just a broken heart. Substance abuse provides temporary enjoyment, but ultimately destroys lives. (As an attorney, I have witnessed this many times).

The writer of Ecclesiastes realized the folly of pleasure when he wrote: "I said to myself, 'Come now, I will test you with pleasure. So enjoy yourself.' And behold, it too was futility. I said of laughter, 'It is madness,' and of pleasure, 'What does it accomplish?' " (Ecclesiastes 2:1-2) The same is true of money, power, sex, and even children. Anything you can name, other than God, will ultimately prove unsatisfying, because the delight of such things does not last.

Now contrast such futility with what Jesus promised for his followers: "I came that they may have life, and have *it* abundantly." (John 10:10) The abundant life is more than just eternal life. When we follow Jesus we find contentment *in this life*, just as Paul said:

> I have learned to be content in whatever circumstances I am. I know how to get along with humble means, and I also know how to live in prosperity.
>
> —Philippians 4:11-12[36]

The follower of Christ learns to trust him and be content with whatever he provides, for we really don't *need* anything else. This is not to imply that Christians don't have fun, because they certainly do. However, they have realized that lasting relationships—with God and others—built on trust and love are more satisfying than the pursuit of temporary pleasures.

Contentment is what the godless person seldom finds. And if she does find it, it will prove maddeningly transitory, because it necessarily depends upon the ever-changing people or things of this earthly life. Contentment cannot last apart from God. It is "vanity and striving after wind." (Ecclesiastes 2:11)

God's ways are the ways of contentment, abundant life, and eternal life. Satan's ways are the ways of temporary pleasure, futility, and death. Only a fool would prefer the latter over the former.[37] Those who contend that Satan's ways are better or more fun are promoting a lie. Experience will eventually show them that, like Eve, they have been deceived. The follower of Christ knows a better way.

Ch. 7 – Three Lies People Tell About Satan

Endnotes for Chapter Seven, "Three Lies People Tell About God"

1. Chapter Six of *Beyond Blind Faith: Reasons for the Hope We Have (1 Peter 3:15)* is entitled, "Three Lies People Tell About God."

2. Technically, of course, an untruth uttered without knowledge of its falsity is not really a "lie." However, "Three Untruths People Tell About Satan" just seemed too awkward.

3. For example, see Matthew 4:1-11, in which he is called "the devil" four times and "Satan" once.

4. See Matthew 10:25, 12:27; Mark 3:22; Luke 11:15, 11:18-19.

5. See Revelation 12:3-9 and 20:2.

6. See Matthew 12:26, 13:39, 16:23, 25:41; Mark 1:13, 3:23, 3:26, 4:15, 8:33; Luke 4:2-3, 4:6, 4:13, 8:12, 10:18, 11:18, 13:16, 22:3, 22:31; John 6:70, 8:44, 13:2, 13:27; Acts 5:3, 10:38, 13:10, 26:18; Romans 16:20; 1 Corinthians 5:5, 7:5; 2 Corinthians 2:11, 11:14, 12:7; Ephesians 4:27, 6:11; 1 Thessalonians 2:18; 2 Thessalonians 2:9; 1 Timothy 1:20, 3:6-7, 5:15; 2 Timothy 2:26; Hebrews 2:14; James 4:7; 1 Peter 5:8; 1 John 3:8, 3:10; Jude 9; Revelation 2:9-10, 2:13, 2:24, 3:9, 12:9, 12:12, 20:2, 20:7, 20:10.

7. See 1 Chronicles 21:1; Job 1:6-9, 1:12, 2:2:1-4, 2:6-7; Zechariah 3:1-2.

8. Lived 1933 - 1998

9. See Luke 13:10-16

10. Acts 10:38

11. 2 Corinthians 12:7

12. 1 Thessalonians 2:18

13. Matthew 4:8-9, Luke 4:5-6

14. Job 1:1-19 and 2:1-7

15. For David, see 1 Chronicles 21:1-7. For Judas, see John 13:2. For Ananias, see Acts 5:1-13. For Peter, see Matthew 16:21-23 and Mark 8:31-33.

16. See, for example, how God hardened Pharaoh's heart, in Exodus 4:21, 7:3, 9:12, 10:1, 10:20, 10:27, 11:10, 14:4, and 14:8. Or see Deuteronomy 2:30, Joshua 11:20, and Romans 9:18, each of which makes clear that God can change our desires and actions when necessary to accomplish His purposes.

17. 2 Thessalonians 2:8-10

18. Matthew 4:1-11, Mark 1:12-13, and Luke 4:1-13

19. 1 Corinthians 7:5

20. For example, the *American Standard Version*, the *New King James Version*, and the *Bible in Basic English* all translate Matthew 6:13 this way.

21. Ephesians 4:25-27

22. 1 Timothy 3:7; 2 Timothy 2:24-26

23. Ephesians 6:10-13

24. Matthew 22:36-38; Mark 12:28-30; Luke 10:25-28

25. John 13:34-35

26. See also Mark 28:31 and Luke 10:25-28.

27. See Luke 10:29-37

28. John 8:44

29. Ephesians 4:26-27

30. Acts 13:10; 2 Thessalonians 2:9-10; Revelation 12:3-9, 20:2-3, 20:7-10

31. Revelation 2:20-24

32. 2 Corinthians 11:13-15

33. Acts 13:10, 26:18

34. 1 John 3:8; see also, 1 John 3:10

35. 2 Thessalonians 2:12

36. See also, 1 Timothy 6:6-8 and Hebrews 13:5, which also speak of contentment.

37. See Psalm 14:1 and Psalm 53:1.

Chapter 8
YOU DON'T DESERVE THIS

Most of us don't think we deserve "bad" things in life. In fact, one of the most common arguments against the existence of God is that "bad" things happen—to people we respect, to people we love, and of course to us. If God exists, so the argument goes, he wouldn't allow these "bad" things to happen.[1] The unspoken assumption is that we *deserve* better. However, as common and as understandable as this assumption may be, from God's perspective it is simply wrong.

To see what I mean, imagine that you are a judge and a friend of yours is guilty of stealing $50. Your duty is to punish her in accordance with the law. Will you let her off? Can you do so without acting unjustly and violating your oath to enforce the law fairly? After all, she did break the law. If you don't punish her, how can you justly punish a person who stole $100? or $100,000? If you let her get away with stealing $50, then the law becomes a lie. The letter of the law has no room for exceptions, and the fact that other people do the same, or worse, is not (and cannot be) a defense. Even if your friend only stole $5, she still broke the law and she deserves some type of punishment.

That is God's dilemma. He cannot let any of us off the hook without being unjust. After all, he commanded us not to steal.[2] He didn't say, "Don't steal more than $50." If he doesn't punish you because you stole less than someone else, where does he draw the line? Someone could justifiably say, "I'm not really any worse than that fellow. We *both* stole. Why does he get off and I don't?"

Furthermore, God's dilemma is much worse than that of the judge, for God sees *all* of our offenses, including those we hide from other people. To remain just, he must punish us for those offenses, too, no matter how minor. (However, this does not mean that God punishes us in this Earthly life,[3] or that such punishment consists of eternal torture in Hell.[4])

If we wish to avoid punishment, one way is to obey God's laws. But we must obey every law, and we must do so all of the time, because God sees our every misstep. In other words, we must be perfect. Paul put it this way:

> For as many as are of the works of the Law are under a curse; for it is written, "CURSED IS EVERYONE WHO DOES NOT ABIDE BY ALL THINGS WRITTEN IN THE BOOK OF THE LAW, TO PERFORM THEM."
>
> —Galatians 3:10[5]

James makes the same point when he says: "For whoever keeps the whole law and yet stumbles in one *point*, he has become guilty of all." (James 2:10)[6]

Of course, none of us can truly attain this standard of perfection: "for all have sinned and fall short of the glory of God." (Romans 3:23)[7] As John says: "If we say that we have no sin, we are deceiving ourselves and the truth is not in us." (1 John 1:8) Peter recognized that the Israelites had never been able to scrupulously obey all of God's laws, so he insisted that the Gentile Christians not be subjected to this impossible burden.[8]

If you are so egotistical that you think you can actually measure up to God's standards, read Jesus' Sermon on the Mount,[9] where he sets forth impossibly high standards for our behavior, such as: rejoice and be glad when you are insulted, persecuted, and lied about;[10] do not even be angry with other people, much less insult them;[11] do not lust after a woman who is not your wife (or a man who is not your husband);[12] don't get divorced except in very limited circumstances;[13] if someone hits you, do not hit back, but turn the other cheek;[14] "love your enemies and pray for those who persecute you" (Matthew 5:44);[15] practice your religion privately, trusting God, rather than men, to recognize your piety;[16] do not worry about food or money or material possessions—instead, trust God to provide all that you need;[17] do not concern yourself with the transgressions of others, but merely worry about your own behavior.[18]

Adam and Eve gave in to temptation, and we have much more in common with them than we would really care to admit. As the saying goes, "I can resist anything but temptation." We all have our weaknesses, and we all have moments when we would prefer that God not be watching or listening. But of course, he is always watching and listening. And since none of us measures up to God's standards, our imperfections result in wrath:

> For the wrath of God is revealed from heaven against all ungodliness and unrighteousness of men who suppress the truth in unrighteousness.
>
> —Romans 1:18[19]

Note that God's anger is directed against *all* ungodliness and unrighteousness, not merely against those more wicked than ourselves. We may not like it, but all of us are "by nature children of wrath." (Ephesians 2:3) We deserve God's anger because we have hurt and offended others— and by hurting and offending his children, we have hurt and

offended God. Like disobedient children or convicted criminals, we deserve to be punished. In fact, the New Testament
says we deserve death.[20]

Fortunately, God does not want to give us what we
deserve. That is why Jesus came, to save us from God's
wrath:

> But God demonstrates His own love toward
> us, in that while we were yet sinners, Christ
> died for us. Much more then, having now been
> justified by His blood, we shall be saved from
> the wrath *of God* through Him. For if while we
> were enemies we were reconciled to God
> through the death of His Son, much more, hav-
> ing been reconciled, we shall be saved by His
> life.
>
> —Romans 5:8-10[21]

Christ saves us from God's wrath, not because we deserve it,[22] but because he loves us and wants to rescue us.
This is what the New Testament means when it says we are
saved by "grace," which means "unmerited favor."[23] Salvation is God's free gift.[24] We don't deserve it, and we don't
have to earn it—we just need to accept it.

Since we have not given God anything that wasn't his
already, he doesn't *owe* us anything. So don't get mad at God
when calamity or misfortune strikes, as if he owed you a duty to prevent it. Instead, recognize that whatever good things
you receive from him are much more than you deserve. And
be grateful for the greatest gift he could possibly give you—
salvation leading to eternal life. He loves you, and wants to
give it to you, even though you don't deserve it.

Endnotes for Chapter Eight, "You Don't Deserve This"

1. For more on this topic, see Chapter Three of my book, *Beyond Blind Faith*, entitled "Why Do Bad Things Happen (to Me)?"

2. See Exodus 20:15, Leviticus 19:11, and Deuteronomy 5:19.

3. This topic is discussed in my book, *Beyond Blind Faith*, Chapter Six, "Three Lies People Tell About God."

4. This topic is discussed in my book, *Beyond Blind Faith*, Chapter Five, "What Hell Is Really Like."

5. See also Romans 10:5. The capital letters in Galatians 3:10 are a quotation from the Old Testament. See Deuteronomy 27:26.

6. See also, Romans 2:12, Galatians 5:3, and Matthew 5:17-20.

7. See also, Romans 3:9-12.

8. See Acts 15:7-10.

9. Matthew, chapters 5 through 7

10. Matthew 5:11-12

11. Matthew 5:22

12. Matthew 5:28

13. Matthew 5:32

14. Matthew 5:39

15. See also, Luke 6:27-28.

16. Matthew 6:1-18

17. Matthew 6:24-34

18. Matthew 7:1-5; many other examples could be cited to demonstrate God's standards and how difficult they are to meet, such as: Romans 1:29-31; 1 Corinthians 6:9-11; Galatians; 5:19-21; Ephesians 5:5-6; Philippians 3:18-19; Colossians 3:5-6; Revelation 21:8, 22:15.

19. See also Romans 2:5-6 and 2:8.

20. Romans 8:13; see also Romans 1:32, 6:20-21, 6:23, 7:5, 7:22-24, 8:6, 8:13; 2 Corinthians 7:10; James 1:14-15, 5:19-20; 1 John 3:14-15; Revelation 21:8.

21. See also, for example, Matthew 26:27-28; Mark 10:45; John 3:14-17, 6:51-58; Romans 8:1-4; Ephesians 5:2; 1 Thessalonians 1:10; 1 Timothy 1:15, 2:5-6; Hebrews 9:26-28, 10:10-14; 1 Peter 3:18.

22. See for example, Romans 11:6 or Ephesians 2:8-9. See also, Luke 1:76-78 and Titus 3:5-7.

23. See, for example, Ephesians 2:4-6; see also, Acts 15:11, 20:32; Romans 3:24, 5:15, 11:6; Galatians 2:21, 5:4; Ephesians 1:7, 2:8-9; 1 Timothy 2:14; 2 Timothy 1:9; Titus 2:11, 3:5-7; Hebrews 4:16.

24. See Romans 3:24, 5:15-17, 6:23; Ephesians 2:8.

Chapter 9
LET'S TALK ABOUT SEX

God is Okay With Sex—Yes, Really! Christians have a reputation—not altogether undeserved, I must admit—for being uptight about sex. So let's get one thing straight: God is very much in favor of sex. After all, it was his idea:

> God created man in His own image, in the image of God He created him; male and female He created them. God blessed them; and God said to them, "Be fruitful and multiply, and fill the earth."
>
> —Genesis 1:27-28

A whole book of the Bible—Song of Solomon—is devoted to the subject of the physical attraction between man and woman.[1] Nor does the Bible support the idea that God intended sex only for procreation. Even that old prude Paul warned married couples not to abstain from sexual relations, except occasionally and for short periods of time, because the sexual attraction is too strong:

> The husband must fulfill his duty to his wife, and likewise also the wife to her husband. The wife does not have authority over her own body, but the husband *does;* and likewise also the husband does not have authority over his own body, but the wife *does.* Stop depriving one another, except by agreement for a time, so that you may devote yourselves to prayer, and come together again so that Satan will not tempt you because of your lack of self-control.
>
> —1 Corinthians 7:3-5[2]

73

Paul was unmarried, and he considered that state preferable to marriage, since he had no wife to distract him from devotion to God.[3] Yet Paul recognized the reality of sexual desires, and he endorsed marriage as the way to give expression to those desires.[4] The idea that God frowns on sex, or that he approves of it only for making babies, finds no support in the Bible.

However, the Bible does prohibit various types of sex outside of the marriage relationship. Adultery is probably foremost on this list, since it is condemned in both the Old and New Testaments, and even has a place in the Ten Commandments.[5] Bestiality is also forbidden,[6] as is incest[7] and rape.[8] Homosexual conduct—as controversial as this has become—must also be included on this list, since both the Old and New Testaments denounce it.[9] The punishment in the Old Testament for each of these sexual offenses was death. Consensual sexual intercourse by an unmarried man with an unmarried woman was also forbidden, but carried only a "life sentence"—the man was required to marry her, if her father would permit it.[10]

To Judge or Not to Judge. With that said, what should be the proper attitude of a Christian toward those who violate these rules regarding sex? That depends on the status of the offender, as Paul points out in his first letter to the church at Corinth:

> I wrote you in my letter not to associate with immoral people; I *did* not at all *mean* with the immoral people of this world, or with the covetous and swindlers, or with idolaters, for then you would have to go out of the world. But actually, I wrote to you not to associate

with any so-called brother if he is an immoral person, or covetous, or an idolater, or a reviler, or a drunkard, or a swindler—not even to eat with such a one. For what have I to do with judging outsiders? Do you not judge those who are within *the church?* But those who are outside, God judges.

—1 Corinthians 5:9-13

In the Corinthian church, one of its members was committing adultery with his step-mother.[11] Since Paul learned of it in Ephesus, where he wrote 1 Corinthians, the man was apparently making no effort to conceal the affair—nor were the Corinthians.[12] Paul ordered the Corinthians to kick this man out of the church, so that others would not be led astray by his wickedness.[13]

Like Paul, we must concern ourselves with open and obvious wrongdoing *within the church*, lest it spread like a contagious disease. Jesus makes the same point in Matthew 18:15-17:

If your brother sins,[14] go and show him his fault in private; if he listens to you, you have won your brother. But if he does not listen *to you*, take one or two more with you, so that BY THE MOUTH OF TWO OR THREE WITNESSES EVERY FACT MAY BE CONFIRMED. If he refuses to listen to them, tell it to the church; and if he refuses to listen even to the church, let him be to you as a Gentile and a tax collector.[15]

Beyond Shallow Faith

On the other hand, the behavior of non-Christians is God's concern, not ours. The words of Jesus echo this sentiment, as he warned us against judging others:

> Do not judge so that you will not be judged.
> For in the way you judge, you will be judged;
> and by your standard of measure, it will be
> measured to you.
>
> —Matthew 7:1-2[16]

The humorous image of a man with a log in his eye attempting to remove a speck from his brother's eye[17] effectively communicates the truth that we should be more concerned about our own behavior than the behavior of others. Jesus' approach toward ordinary sinners was to freely associate with them and try to lead them to God.[18] The lesson for Christians is that we should not judge those who are outside the church. Jude 22-23 explains that even when we are revolted by someone's sin, we should be gentle and merciful toward the sinner.

But when someone *within the church* openly practices sin, or openly advocates it, then we are forced to act, not only for the good of the sinner, but for others whom he might lead astray. The sinner must be confronted and, if he refuses to repent and change, then, as Jesus said, "let him be to you as a Gentile and a tax collector." (Matthew 18:17) This means that he is no longer part of the church body—he is excluded from the assembly and from communion—but it does not mean that we should break all ties with him. Jesus treated Gentiles and tax collectors with patience and kindness, seeking to lead them to repentance without imitating their deeds. That is how we should treat an unrepentant Christian who openly misbehaves, sexually or otherwise.

Such treatment fits well with the second greatest commandment, which is, "You shall love your neighbor as yourself." (Matthew 22:39)[19] The parable of the Good Samaritan[20] reminds us that everyone is our neighbor. So we must be kind to all people—even those whom society tells us to shun.

Advice for the Honest Christian. In our culture today, many disagree with some of what the Bible says about sex. They see nothing wrong with sex between consenting adults, whether or not they are married, and even if they are of the same sex. How should we respond as Christians? First, to the extent that these people are outside the church, our response is simply to treat them with as much love, kindness, and patience as we can. As Paul and Jesus said, God is their judge—we are not.

But what advice can we offer the Christian who is honestly torn between the sexual longings he feels and his desire to obey God? First, God knows much better than we do what is good for us, and what is not, and we tread on very thin ice when we think we know more than God. Our "enlightened" society has led to dramatic increases in divorce and unmarried pregnancies since the 1950s.

Studies cast doubt on the wisdom of such enlightenment. They tell us that children who grow up with two married parents generally do better on measures of adjustment, development, and well-being.[21] Similar studies reveal that children who grow up with a father are, on average, better adjusted in the areas of sex-role and gender-identity development, school performance, psychosocial adjustment, and perhaps control of aggression.[22]

The "sexual revolution" of the 1960s led to greater problems with sexually transmitted diseases, which spread

77

more rapidly and more extensively when people routinely have multiple sexual partners, be they heterosexual or homosexual. And I need hardly point out the devastating effects of adultery, which shatters the trust which is essential to any good marriage.

God didn't make rules about sex because he wanted to punish us or deprive us of something fun, but because he wanted to protect us—and, perhaps more importantly, our children and our sexual partners—from the potentially adverse consequences of sexual misconduct. Violating God's rules about sex is a terribly selfish thing to do. We sacrifice the feelings and the welfare of others for the sake of our momentary pleasure. God expects more from Christians.

So God tells unmarried Christians to remain celibate[23] until and unless they get married, while married Christians must confine themselves to sexual relations within the marriage relationship. To do otherwise is to elevate our own selfish pleasures above God's commands. Doing so jeopardizes our relationship with God, who insists that we love him and others more than ourselves.[24]

But what about homosexuals? If, as most homosexuals contend (and I have no reason to doubt), their inborn sexual attraction is toward persons of the same sex,[25] and they have no sexual interest in members of the opposite sex, is God really telling homosexual Christians that they shouldn't engage in sex with consenting adults to whom they are naturally attracted? I believe the answer must be "Yes."

Inborn sexual attraction is irrelevant, for God does not forbid the attraction, but the action. Nor is the action excused by the attraction, as our society recognizes by criminalizing sexual relations with minors, animals, and close relatives regardless of any natural sexual motivation. I recognize, of course, that most homosexual conduct is between consenting adults, but this does not excuse it either. Adultery, incest, and sex outside of marriage often involve consenting adults, too, but God condemns them nonetheless.

Where did we ever get this misguided notion that sexual activity is a God-given right? Our society places many limits on sexual conduct, and so does God. We place ourselves at risk when we transgress either one. And after all, celibacy is not a death sentence. For the past 2,000 years, Christian monks, nuns, priests, and others have voluntarily adopted an unmarried and celibate lifestyle through a desire to get closer to God—just as Paul did.

Sex Offenders in Heaven? Nevertheless, I do not say that a Christian who has engaged—or even who continues to engage—in sexual misconduct cannot be saved and reach Heaven. God, not I, will judge such matters. And I ask this of Christians who insist otherwise: why are sexual offenses different?

As we discussed in Chapter Eight ("You Don't Deserve This"), Jesus' Sermon on the Mount[26] lays down a moral standard that is impossible to fully meet. Even Paul, who was a giant in the faith, admitted that he was not perfect,[27] and boldly asserted that "all have sinned and fall short of the glory of God." (Romans 3:23)

While not retreating from the position that sexual misconduct is wrong, I have long wondered why many Christians seem to consider sexual offenses so different from sins such as greed, envy, strife, deceit, malice, gossip, slander, arrogance, boasting, disobedience to parents, and untrustworthiness;[28] fornication, idolatry, theft, covetousness, drunkenness, reviling, and dishonesty;[29] murder, kidnapping, lying, perjury, "and whatever else is contrary to sound teaching." (1 Timothy 1:9-10 and 9:10) Has there ever been a Christian other than Christ who successfully eliminated all of these faults from his life? Add to that the list in the Sermon on the Mount, as well sins of omission (such as neglecting the sick and the needy),[30] and none of us has any cause to be self-righteous or judgmental.

The story of the woman caught in adultery[31] illustrates the point that none of us is without sin. When the Jewish leaders brought the woman to Jesus and demanded that she be stoned in accordance with Jewish law, Jesus replied: "He who is without sin among you, let him *be the* first to throw a stone at her." (John 8:7) One by one, her accusers all left, recognizing that none of them was sinless.

Paul makes the same point repeatedly in his Letter to the Romans,[32] and also gives this warning: "Therefore you have no excuse, everyone of you who passes judgment, for in that which you judge another, you condemn yourself; for you who judge practice the same things." (Romans 2:1)

Indeed, sexual offenses might be the least egregious sins of all. In Heaven, Jesus tells us, marriage will be abolished.[33] Presumably, therefore, no procreation or sexual relations will be possible anymore. Both the opportunity and the temptation to engage in sexual misconduct will be eliminated. Yet such sins as hatred, anger, arrogance, and lying could still cause problems. So shouldn't God be more concerned about the latter than the former when he decides who gets into Heaven?

If you are a Christian who cannot conceive of a homosexual or a child molester getting into Heaven, consider Jesus' parable of the Pharisee and the tax-collector who go to the temple to pray.[34] In many ways, the tax-collectors of Jesus' day were treated like the sex offenders of today. People who considered themselves righteous—as well as many who did not— hated and shunned them.[35] Yet in Jesus' parable, the tax-collector who seeks God's mercy receives it, while the self-righteous Pharisee does not. Note that Jesus did not say that the tax-collector stopped sinning, or even that he stopped being a tax-collector—only that he humbled himself before God and received mercy. Luke's commentary on this parable is enlightening: "He also told this parable to some people who trusted in themselves that they were righteous, and viewed others with contempt." (Luke 18:9)

Jesus seldom got angry, but when he did he directed his anger at the unmerciful and the self-righteous.[36] When the Pharisees criticized him for associating with tax collectors and sinners, he rebuked them.[37] Those of us who self-righteously condemn "sinners" would do well to imitate the humility of the tax collector in Jesus' parable[38] rather than the arrogance and conceit of the Pharisee.

Good Works and Bad Deeds. Of course, I do not believe Christians should intentionally commit sexual misconduct, or that God is happy when we do. As Paul says in his letter to the Romans:

> What shall we say then? Are we to continue in
> sin so that grace may increase? May it never
> be! How shall we who died to sin still live in it?
>
> —Romans 6:2[39]

But Paul makes the point in Romans that we cannot *earn* salvation. Instead, God bestows it as a free gift on those who love and trust him.[40]

All of our good works and righteous living count as nothing when it comes to salvation. Isaiah says, "all our righteous deeds are like a filthy garment" (Isaiah 64:6), because we can never be good enough to merit salvation through our own efforts. God's standards are simply too high: "For whoever keeps the whole law and yet stumbles in one *point,* he has become guilty of all." (James 2:10)

If you have *ever* lied, stolen, or gossiped, or been dishonest, envious, arrogant, or greedy (and who hasn't?), then you are just as guilty in God's eyes as the worst adulterer or sex offender. We will not get into Heaven because we have done anything to deserve it, but because of our devotion to him.[41]

If our good works cannot get us into Heaven, will our bad deeds keep us out? The answer, I believe, must be a qualified "no." Our heart, not our deeds, is what matters to God. So long as our heart remains true to God, our deeds matter little or not at all. Consider what Jesus says: "But give that which is within as charity, and then all things are clean for you." (Luke 11:41) Jesus, who was careful with his words, did not merely say "all foods," but "all things." Paul makes a similar point, more than once.[42] If "all things" are clean, does that include sexual misconduct? Or does "all" not really mean "all"?

Are Sexual Sins Different? I concede that evil deeds— and especially those which are deliberate—can lead us away from God and corrupt our heart's devotion to him. That corruption can in turn endanger our relationship with God and, I think, jeopardize our salvation. Nevertheless, I don't believe most Christians would argue the point that none of us is perfect, and that God will forgive our imperfections if our heart is devoted to him. That is basic Christianity. Yet some of these same Christians who seek and accept God's mercy for their own faults seem unwilling to extend the same mercy to those who are guilty of sexual misbehavior. Why are sexual sins different from all other sins? I find nothing in the Bible that says they are.

The New Testament consistently teaches that any person who becomes a Christian should to try to avoid sin and eliminate it from their lives, whether that sin be envy, greed, lying, arrogance, etc. And we cannot ignore the admonitions of Paul and Jesus that we must never tolerate manifest, unrepentant sin within the church.[43] Any Christian who openly encourages murder or divorce or lying, or any other sinful conduct, would have to be confronted about it. Similarly, a Christian who overtly practices or advocates sexual behavior which the Bible says is wrong must be opposed according to the model Jesus outlines in Matthew 18:15-17.

In such an encounter, we must be careful about our own motives and actions. "Judgment" in this context has nothing to do with condemnation or punishment—that is God's job, not ours. Thus, Paul tells us not to judge those outside the church.[44] Instead, the purpose of judgment in this context is *always* to help our fellow Christians—the brother or sister who is going astray, as well as the Christians who are in danger of being led into sin by them. We must carry out this duty in love and humility, keeping in mind that we too are sinners, and that we are no more precious in God's eyes than the person whom we are trying to help. Our purpose must be to turn the sinning brother back to God's ways—or perhaps, more accurately, to persuade him to repent and turn himself back.

On the other hand, the Christian who is trying not to sin, but who sometimes succumbs to temptation, sexual or otherwise, is *not* the type of person we should be judging. She needs our prayers, our assistance, our encouragement, and our efforts to help her mature spiritually, but not our judgment. As Paul said, "Who are you to judge the servant of another? To his own master he stands or falls; and he will stand, for the Lord is able to make him stand." (Romans 14:4)

Endnotes for Chapter Nine, "Let's Talk About Sex"

1. For example, in Song of Solomon 7:1-4, the groom admires his bride's many attractive physical features. See also Song of Solomon 1:2, 2:2, 2:14, 4:1-5, 4:7, 4:9-16, 5:1, 5:4, 5:8, 5:10-16, 6:3-7, 7:5-12, and 8:6-7.

2. Note that Paul calls marital sexual relations a *duty*.

3. See 1 Corinthians 7:1, 7:7-8, 7:32-40.

4. See 1 Corinthians 7:2, 7:9; 1 Timothy 5:11-12, 5:14.

5. See Exodus 20:14 and Deuteronomy 5:18. Adultery is also condemned elsewhere, such as: Leviticus 18:20, 20:10; Deuteronomy 22:22; Proverbs 6:32-35; Jeremiah 5:7-8, 7:9-10, 23:14, 29:21-23; Hosea 4:2; Matthew 5:27, 19:17-18; Mark 10:17-19; Luke 18:18-20; Romans 13:9-10; James 2:11. Deuteronomy 22:23-24 should probably be included in this list as well, since it addresses sexual intercourse with a girl who is engaged to be married. God uses adultery as a metaphor for the unfaithfulness of His people, who chased after false gods instead of remaining faithful to the "Husband" who made a covenant with them. See, for example, Jeremiah 3:6-9; Ezekiel 16:32-39, 23:36-39; Hosea 1:2, 2:1-8, 4:12-13; Revelation 2:20-22.

6. Exodus 22:19; Leviticus 18:23, 20:15-16; Deuteronomy 27:21

7. Leviticus 20:11-12, 20:14, 20:17, 20:19-21; Deuteronomy 22:30, 27:20, 27:22-23

8. Deuteronomy 22:25-27

9. See Leviticus 18:22, 20:13; Romans 1:26-27; 1 Corinthians 6:9; and 1 Timothy 1:10.

10. Exodus 22:16-17; Deuteronomy 22:28-29 is similar, and adds that he may not divorce her.

11. 1 Corinthians 5:1

12. Paul accuses the Corinthians of being arrogant and boastful about this immorality (1 Corinthians 5:2 and 5:6). Perhaps the offender was wealthy or a man of some importance.

13. 1 Corinthians 5:6-8 and 5:13.

14. In simple terms, "sin" means to fall short of what God wants us to be. See Romans 3:23.

15. The language in all-capitals is a quote from Deuteronomy 19:15; see also Deuteronomy 17:6.

16. See also Luke 6:37-38.

17. Matthew 7:3-5; Luke 6:41-42

18. See Matthew 9:10-13, 11:19; Mark 2:15-17; Luke 5:29-32, 7:34, 15:1-32.

19. See also, Mark 12:31, Luke 10:27, and Leviticus 19:18.

20. Luke 10:25-37

21. Lamb, *The Role of the Father in Child Development*, Chapter 12, "The Effects of Divorce on Fathers and Children," by Paul R. Amato and Julie M. Sobolewski, p. 342.

22. Lamb, *The Role of the Father in Child Development*, Chapter 1, "The Role of the Father: *An Introduction*," by Michael E. Lamb and Catherine S. Ta-mis-Lemonda, pp. 6 and 16.

23. Masturbation can provide a sexual outlet for those who are celibate, and the contention of some that the Bible prohibits masturbation is simply wrong. The sixty-six books of the Bible do not even mention the word. The fallacy that masturbation is prohibited by the Bible is allegedly based on the story of Onan in Genesis. (See Genesis 38:6-10.) Onan was the brother of Er, who was the husband of Tamar. Er died before he and Tamar had any children. In this situation, Israelite custom required Onan to provide children for his deceased brother by impregnating Er's wife, Tamar. (Genesis 38:8. See also Deuteronomy 25:5-10.) Apparently Onan didn't like this custom, because he ejaculated onto the ground instead of into Tamar's womb. (Genesis 38:9) As a result, God killed him. (Genesis 38:10) But what Onan did was not masturbation, but *coitus interruptus*—stopping sexual intercourse before he ejaculated, in an effort to avoid getting Tamar pregnant.

24. See Mark 12:28-31, Matthew 22:36-39, Luke 10:27, and Luke 14:25-26. The message of these verses—and indeed, the overriding message of both the Old and New Testaments—is that God must be of first importance in our lives.

25. I do not believe that most homosexuals *choose* to be attracted to members of their own sex, any more than I choose to be attracted to women.

26. Matthew 5:1-7:29

27. See Philippians 3:12.

28. See Romans 1:28-31.

29. See 1 Corinthians 6:9-10.

30. See Matthew 25:31-46, and especially verses 44-45.

31. John 8:3-11. This story is not contained in the oldest manuscripts of John's gospel, but it is so consistent with Jesus' character and teachings that I believe it must be based on an actual event.

32. See, for example, Romans 2:1-8, 3:9-12, and 3:23.

33. See Matthew 22:30 and Mark 12:25.

34. Luke 18:9-14

35. The tax-collectors in Palestine were actually Jews who collected Roman taxes. The Romans required the tax-collectors to pay a certain amount to Rome, and they could keep whatever money they collected in excess of that amount. Thus, the tax-collectors were viewed as collaborators with the hated and oppressive Romans. In addition, many of the tax-collectors were corrupt, and became wealthy by cheating their fellow Jews.

36. See, for example, Matthew 12:9-34, 23:1-33; Mark 3:1-5; Luke 13:10-16. Similarly, Jesus' righteous anger when he cleansed the Temple of those who were cheating people in the name of religion (Luke 19:45-46; Mark 11:15-17; Matthew 21:12-13) appears to have been directed primarily at the Jewish leaders who permitted it, as we see from their reaction: "The chief priests and the scribes heard *this*, and *began* seeking how to destroy Him." (Mark 11:18; see also Luke 19:47)

37. See Matthew 9:12-13, Mark 2:15-17, and Luke 5:29-32.

38. Luke 18:9-14

39. See also Romans 3:7-8 and Romans 3:15-16.

40. See, for example, Romans 3:21-24. As I discuss in Chapter Ten ("Is Free Will an Illusion?"), the English words "faith" and "believe" translate the Greek word, *pisteuô* (or the noun form, *pistis*), which means to trust God, to rely on him, and to make a strong personal commitment to him—i.e., to surrender our lives to him.

41. See Romans 4:4-5 and Philippians 3:8-9.

42. See 1 Corinthians 6:12 and 10:23. See also Titus 1:15 and Romans 14:14.

43. 1 Corinthians 5:1-13; Matthew 18:15-17

44. 1 Corinthians 5:9-10, 12

Chapter 10
IS FREE WILL AN ILLUSION?

So Jesus was saying to those Jews who had believed Him, "If you continue in My word, *then* you are truly disciples of Mine; and you will know the truth, and the truth will make you free."

—John 8:31-32

A mouse lives in a tiny corner of the earth and knows nothing of the greater world beyond her small territory. Her nature drives her to find food, reproduce, and raise baby mice. She cannot change what God made her or where he put her.

We are like the mouse in many ways. We do not choose the time, the place, or the circumstances of our birth. Our nature drives us to eat and sleep—we cannot choose to do otherwise for any extended period of time without serious consequences. The almost irresistible attraction of the opposite sex compels most of us to mate and reproduce. And as much as we pretend otherwise, none of us can avoid death.[1] Yet something inside us cries out that we are different from the mouse. We believe we can rise above our circumstances and resist our nature. We can *choose* how we act. We are *free*. Or are we?

Some argue that our freedom is simply an illusion. Our choices are all determined by some combination of genetics, circumstances, experiences, and environment, leaving no room for free will. For example, many of us "choose" a religion because our culture or our parents ingrained it in us as children.[2]

Among Christians, some argue that freedom to choose our eternal destiny is similarly illusory—i.e., that God decided whether you and I would go to Heaven or Hell[3] before we were even born. Such giants of the faith as St. Augustine,[4] John Calvin, and John Knox[5] have advocated this position. Many others, reading the same Bible, have concluded that our eternal fate depends upon our choices. But what does the Bible say?

The Case for Free Will

Some degree of freedom of action seems to be implicit in the New Testament. When Jesus says, "follow Me," as he often does,[6] the statement suggests that the hearer can choose to either follow him or not. And while most chose to follow, the rich young ruler did not.[7] When Jesus tells someone to go somewhere,[8] or to do something,[9] he does not even hint that the person lacks the freedom to do otherwise—and as with the rich young ruler, occasionally a person did do otherwise.[10] Jesus himself seems to have been at least a little surprised when the people of his home town of Nazareth rejected him,[11] for "He wondered at their unbelief." (Mark 6:6)

More to the point, the New Testament is full of commands and pleas regarding how we *ought* to behave. For example, Jesus talks about the need to humble ourselves.[12] He admonishes us not to judge other people,[13] but instead to forgive them.[14] He forbids divorce under most circumstances.[15] He warns against the dangers of money and greed, and insists that we should be more concerned about God than about the worries of this life.[16] He urges us to show each other love and kindness.[17] And of course he commands us to think, speak, and act properly, rather than wickedly.[18] Indeed, Jesus' teachings constantly presume that our actions and our *choices* affect our relationship with God,[19] and therefore we must choose wisely.

The teachings of his followers are no different. Very early in the life of the Church, the leaders sent a letter to the Christians in Antioch, setting down a few simple rules for the Gentile Christians there to follow:

> For it seemed good to the Holy Spirit and to us to lay upon you no greater burden than these essentials: that you abstain from things sacrificed to idols and from blood and from things strangled and from fornication; if you keep yourselves free from such things, you will do well.
>
> —Acts 15:28-29[20]

Why write such a letter unless the Antioch Christians were free to conform their conduct to these rules—or choose not to do so?

Similarly, during Paul's first missionary journey, he issues a warning to Elymas the magician that is just silly-stupid unless Elymas actually possessed the freedom to change his behavior:

> You who are full of all deceit and fraud, you son of the devil, you enemy of all righteousness, will you not cease to make crooked the straight ways of the Lord?
>
> —Acts 13:10

Indeed, Paul speaks often of the need to behave properly, perhaps nowhere more clearly than in Romans:

> *Let* love *be* without hypocrisy. Abhor what is evil; cling to what is good. *Be* devoted to one another in brotherly love; give preference to one another in honor; not lagging behind in diligence, fervent in spirit, serving the Lord; rejoicing in hope, persevering in tribulation, devoted to prayer, contributing to the needs of the saints, practicing hospitality.
>
> —Romans 12:9-13[21]

Echoing the teachings of Jesus in the Gospels, the authors of the other New Testament books constantly tell us how we ought to behave. They warn us not to judge others,[22] but instead to think and act with humility.[23] They advise us to be kind, considerate, and forgiving,[24] and to exercise self-control, rather than indulging selfishness, immorality, or other evil desires.[25] They counsel against divorce.[26] They command that we respect and obey those in positions of authority over us.[27] And above all, Jesus' followers implore us to love each other and get along with each other.[28] This is not a complete list of verses that talk about our behavior,[29] but I'm sure you get the idea.

Since Jesus and the New Testament writers tell us how we should behave—on many topics, and with great frequency—they must have believed that we possess some measure of freedom to act accordingly. Yet the New Testament contains even stronger evidence for free will.

I Repent, Therefore I Am Free

The New Testament's terminology regarding how we establish and nurture our relationship with God is especially revealing. Jesus and the New Testament writers use such terms as *repent, love, faith,* and *believe,* all of which involve *choices.*

Jesus' earliest preaching stressed repentance: "From that time [the arrest of John the Baptist] Jesus began to preach and say, 'Repent, for the kingdom of heaven is at hand.' " (Matthew 4:17)[30] John the Baptist delivered a similar message: "John the Baptist appeared in the wilderness preaching a baptism of repentance for the forgiveness of sins." (Mark 1:4)[31] And so did Peter.[32] Indeed, the value and importance of repentance is a constant theme in the New Testament.[33]

To "repent" means to feel sorry for the wrongs you have done,[34] to God and to other people. But in the New Testament it means much more—a point John the Baptist made when he addressed the Jewish religious leaders who came to hear him preach:

> But when he saw many of the Pharisees and Sadducees coming for baptism, he said to them, "You brood of vipers, who warned you to flee from the wrath to come? Therefore **bear fruit in keeping with repentance**; and do not suppose that you can say to yourselves, 'We have Abraham for our father'; for I say to you that from these stones God is able to raise up children to Abraham."
> —Matthew 3:7-9 (emphasis added in boldface)

Beyond Shallow Faith

Repentance involves changing not only your mind, but your heart, your attitude, and your behavior toward God and other people. Repentance necessarily requires freedom. If we lack the freedom to change—our mind, our attitude, and, yes, even our behavior—then the New Testament writers are foolishly imploring us to do something we cannot do. But we must not stop there.

Agapaô-Love and *Pisteuô*-Faith

Jesus also emphasizes the need to love God. In fact, this is paramount:

> One of the scribes came and heard them arguing, and recognizing that He had answered them well, asked Him, "What commandment is the foremost of all?" Jesus answered, "The foremost is, 'HEAR, O ISRAEL! THE LORD OUR GOD IS ONE LORD; AND YOU SHALL LOVE THE LORD YOUR GOD WITH ALL YOUR HEART, AND WITH ALL YOUR SOUL, AND WITH ALL YOUR MIND, AND WITH ALL YOUR STRENGTH.' The second is this, 'YOU SHALL LOVE YOUR NEIGHBOR AS YOURSELF.' There is no other commandment greater than these."
>
> —Mark 12:28-31[35]

As we saw in Chapter Four ("Our Father"), the word "love" in this verse translates the Greek word *agapaô*, the selfless and self-giving love that always seeks what is best for the person loved.[36] This is the kind of love Paul describes in the famous thirteenth chapter of 1 Corinthians:

> Love is patient, love is kind *and* is not jealous; love does not brag *and* is not arrogant, does not act unbecomingly; it does not seek its own, is not provoked, does not take into account a wrong *suffered,* does not rejoice in unrighteousness, but rejoices with the truth; bears all things, believes all things, hopes all things, endures all things.
>
> —1 Corinthians 13:4-7

This type of love has nothing to do with sexual attraction, emotion, or feelings. *Agapaô*-love is a *choice*. Our emotions may tell us to seek revenge against those who have hurt us, but *agapaô*-love chooses a different path:

> You have heard that it was said, 'YOU SHALL LOVE YOUR NEIGHBOR and hate your enemy.' But I say to you, love your enemies and pray for those who persecute you.
>
> —Matthew 5:43-44[37]

Throughout the New Testament we see this idea of love as a choice rather than a feeling. Jesus spoke of it when he said:

> "He who loves father or mother more than Me is not worthy of Me; and he who loves son or daughter more than Me is not worthy of Me. And he who does not take his cross and follow after Me is not worthy of Me. He who has found his life will lose it, and he who has lost his life for My sake will find it."
>
> —Matthew 10:37-39[38]

Jesus might as well have said, "He who **chooses** father or mother over Me is not worthy of me," for that is essentially what he means. Family is important—which Jesus makes clear elsewhere[39]—but God insists that we make him our number one priority. Similarly, God demands that we choose him rather than the pursuit of power, fame, money,[40] or something else.

Agapaô-love is simply not possible without the freedom to give or withhold it. And neither is faith, another constant theme in the New Testament. Jesus mentions the importance of faith in many of his healings:

> And He said to her, "Daughter, your faith has made you well; go in peace and be healed of your affliction."
>
> —Mark 5:34[41]

He even made it a key to salvation: "And He said to the woman, 'Your faith has saved you; go in peace.' " (Luke 7:50)[42] The author of Hebrews says we cannot please God without faith.[43]

No one stressed the importance of faith more than the great missionary and letter writer, Paul, who asserted that God gives us justification,[44] righteousness, and ultimately eternal life as a result of our faith in Christ.[45] Paul points out that Abraham gained favor with God through his faith, rather than by any moral conduct,[46] and that we receive God's grace (his unmerited favor) in the same way, because of our faith:

> For by grace you have been saved through faith; and that not of yourselves, *it is* the gift of

God; not as a result of works, so that no one may boast.

—Ephesians 2:8-9[47]

In addition to the critical role ascribed to faith,[48] the New Testament also talks often about the importance of belief. For example:

As Moses lifted up the serpent in the wilderness, even so must the Son of Man be lifted up; so that whoever believes will in Him have eternal life. For God so loved the world, that He gave His only begotten Son, that whoever believes in Him shall not perish, but have eternal life.

—John 3:14-16

For I am not ashamed of the gospel, for it is the power of God for salvation to everyone who believes, to the Jew first and also to the Greek.

—Romans 1:16[49]

In the original Greek of the New Testament, "faith" and "belief" are both translated from the Greek word, *pisteuô* (or a derivative of it), which is really closer in meaning to "trust" or "surrender."[50] "Belief" recognizes Truth, but *pisteuô*-faith makes a commitment to that Truth. Like *agapaô*-love, *pisteuô*-faith involves a choice—the choice to place our trust in God, and to put our lives and our eternal future in his hands.

Other New Testament terminology merely reinforces this idea that following God is a choice—in many ways, an ongoing, continuous choice—which of course requires the freedom to choose. For example, we are urged to *confess*[51] and to *endure*.[52] We are told we must *forgive* others if we wish to be forgiven by God,[53] and we are commanded to *obey* God.[54] Such commands would be meaningless without the freedom to choose whether or not to comply.

With such overwhelming biblical evidence that we are free, why do some insist that we are not? Is there any Scriptural evidence for predestination? Indeed there is, and a lot of it.

The Case for Predestination

First, the New Testament contains abundant and irrefutable evidence that many specific people were predestined—including Jesus himself:

> An angel of the Lord appeared to him in a dream, saying, "Joseph, son of David, do not be afraid to take Mary as your wife; for the Child who has been conceived in her is of the Holy Spirit. She will bear a Son; and you shall call His name Jesus, for He will save His people from their sins."
>
> —Matthew 1:20-21[55]

Jesus was destined to suffer and be killed—and then to be resurrected—and he was well aware of it:

> For He was teaching His disciples and telling them, "The Son of Man is to be delivered into the hands of men, and they will kill Him; and when He has been killed, He will rise three days later."
>
> —Mark 9:31[56]

The Gospels imply that Judas Iscariot was, in some sense, predestined to betray Christ, just as Peter would deny him and the other disciples would desert him, because Jesus knew about all of these events before they happened.[57] Paul believed that God had destined him to be God's messenger to the Gentiles,[58] and he was surely correct, for God strong-armed him in the most important decisions of his life—from his conversion on the road to Damascus[59] to his journey to Rome,[60] and many critical decisions in between.[61]

Similarly, God gave many other people in the New Testament little or no choice but to act in accordance with his will, such as: John the Baptist's ministry as preacher and prophet,[62] Lazarus' death and resurrection,[63] Pilate's role in condemning Jesus,[64] or the preaching and persecution of Jesus' disciples.[65] Moreover, God almost forced Paul,[66] the apostle Thomas,[67] and the proconsul Sergius Paulus[68] to believe by confronting them with the undeniably miraculous. Paul implies that God used similar methods to persuade the Thessalonians.[69]

We see examples of predestination in the Old Testament as well. Before Jacob and his twin brother Esau were even born,

> The LORD said to her [their mother, Rebekah], "Two nations are in your womb; And two peoples will be separated from your body; And one people shall be stronger than the other; And the older shall serve the younger."
> —Genesis 25:23[70]

Before any of the ten plagues struck Egypt, God told Moses what would happen:

> "You shall speak all that I command you, and your brother Aaron shall speak to Pharaoh that

> he let the sons of Israel go out of his land. But I
> will harden Pharaoh's heart that I may multip-
> ly My signs and My wonders in the land of
> Egypt. When Pharaoh does not listen to you,
> then I will lay My hand on Egypt and bring out
> My hosts, My people the sons of Israel, from
> the land of Egypt by great judgments."
>
> —Exodus 7:2-4[71]

Psalm 139:16 even suggests that God had predetermined the
day of the psalmist's death:

> Your eyes have seen my unformed substance;
> And in Your book were all written
> The days that were ordained *for me,*
> When as yet there was not one of them.

Election, Parables, and Prophecy

The New Testament often speaks of the "elect," and
of those who are "chosen" or "called" by God.[72] Some of
these verses have nothing to do with salvation[73]—and many
are ambiguous[74]—but a few clearly refer to eternal salvation,
such as:

> When the Gentiles heard this, they *began* rejoic-
> ing and glorifying the word of the Lord; and as
> many as had been appointed to eternal life be-
> lieved.
>
> —Acts 13:48

> But we should always give thanks to God for
> you, brethren beloved by the Lord, because
> God has chosen you from the beginning for
> salvation through sanctification by the Spirit

and faith in the truth. It was for this He called
you through our gospel, that you may gain the
glory of our Lord Jesus Christ.

—2 Thessalonians 2:13-14

After you have suffered for a little while, the
God of all grace, who called you to His eternal
glory in Christ, will Himself perfect, confirm,
strengthen *and* establish you.

—1 Peter 5:10[75]

We can also imply predestination from many other
New Testament verses, with varying degrees of reliability.
Parables compare people to plants,[76] trees,[77] or soil,[78] as if
God forms each of us in a way that allows us to respond to
him—or makes us incapable of doing so. Jesus talks of
people being *unable* to understand God's message,[79] without
really making clear whether this inability stems from their
choices or their nature. And he seems to say that some
people have an advantage over others in being able to hear,
understand, and believe his message.[80] Indeed, he even
speaks of some being "given" to him by God for the purpose
of saving them.[81]

Prophecy also implies predestination. If God knows
what a person is going to do, does that person really possess
the freedom to do otherwise?[82] Similarly, our freedom is limited by God's sovereignty and omnipotence—the fact that
God is ultimately in control of *everything*, as Paul pointed out
to the Athenians:

He made from one *man* every nation of mankind to live on all the face of the earth, having

determined *their* appointed times and the boundaries of their habitation.

—Acts 17:26[83]

Indeed, I'm not sure we can even *want* to return to God unless he takes the initiative:

"No one can come to Me unless the Father who sent Me draws him; and I will raise him up on the last day."

—John 6:44[84]

Reconciling Free Will and Predestination

Having made a strong case for both free will and predestination, we next face the question of whether the two can be reconciled. Admittedly, the task appears difficult, yet it is not impossible. After all, the men who wrote the New Testament were no fools. Luke, the author of Acts and the Gospel which bears his name, was a physician.[85] Paul, the likely author of thirteen of the letters in the New Testament, was an educated Pharisee before his conversion to Christianity.[86] The New Testament authors—each in his own style—present the story of Jesus in a way that is at once appealing, compelling, inspiring, and uncompromising. So if these wise and skilled writers appear to not only contradict each other, but themselves as well, and sometimes within a single sentence,[87] perhaps we have misunderstood their meaning.

God Really Does Predestine Some—But Not All.

First, the biblical evidence compels the conclusion that God can *and does* sometimes place very real limits on people's freedom in order to accomplish his purposes. Pharaoh, Judas Iscariot, and Pontius Pilate all played their role in God's plans, as did many Old Testament prophets and kings, and I cannot confidently say that any of them had much freedom to do otherwise. However, predestination in this context does not refer to eternal destiny. While God used Pharaoh, Judas Iscariot, and Pontius Pilate, the Bible is silent about their ultimate salvation. Perhaps God saved them in the end.[88]

In addition, some persons may truly be predestined for salvation, at least in the sense that God can be very persuasive when he wants to be. He made his truth so plain and obvious to Paul, Thomas, and many of the early Christians that their only real "choice" was to accept it and surrender to God's purposes, or to oppose him from sheer wickedness. This appears to be what Paul has in mind when he speaks of the Thessalonians being "chosen" by God:

> We give thanks to God always for all of you, making mention *of you* in our prayers . . . knowing, brethren beloved by God, *His* choice of you; for our gospel did not come to you in word only, but also in power and in the Holy Spirit and with full conviction; just as you know what kind of men we proved to be among you for your sake.
>
> —1 Thessalonians 1:2, 4-5

The same can be said of verses such as Acts 13:48, 2 Thessalonians 2:13-14, and 1 Peter 5:10, all of which I have quoted above.

Nevertheless, the fact that Paul and others were in some sense predestined for salvation does not mean that the ultimate destiny of the rest of us is similarly fixed. To illustrate this truth, let's look at a very strong assertion of predestination from Paul's letter to the Ephesians:

> Blessed *be* the God and Father of our Lord Jesus Christ, who has blessed us with every spiritual blessing in the heavenly *places* in Christ, just as **He chose us** in Him before the foundation of the world, that we would be holy and blameless before Him. In love **He predestined us** to adoption as sons through Jesus Christ to Himself, according to the kind intention of His will, to the praise of the glory of His grace, which He freely bestowed on us in the Beloved. . . In Him also we have obtained an inheritance, **having been predestined** according to His purpose who works all things after the counsel of His will.
>
> —Ephesians 1:3-6 and 10-11
> (emphasis added via boldface)

Paul talks of people, including himself, being "chosen" and "predestined," and I believe he has eternal salvation in mind.[89] But he is not talking about you or me, a fact he makes clear in the next two verses:

> to the end that **we who were the first to hope in Christ** would be to the praise of His glory. In Him, **you also**, after listening to the message of truth, the gospel of your salvation—having also believed, you were sealed in Him with the Holy Spirit of promise.
>
> —Ephesians 1:12-13
> (emphasis added via boldface)

The predestined are "we who were the first to hope in Christ" (Ephesians 1:12)—that is, the early believers, who were Jews. You and I are like the Ephesians—the "you also" of Ephesians 1:13—who come to Christ not through predestination, but by "listening to the message of truth" and embracing it.[90] Thus, although God predestined some early believers for salvation—at least in the sense that he demonstrated the truth of the Gospel to them through indisputable proofs—he gave many others a very real choice. And that latter group includes most of the rest of us.

God's Chosen People. Like the first chapter of Ephesians, chapters 8 and 9 of Paul's Letter to the Romans contain language that strongly supports predestination:

> And we know that God causes all things to work together for good to those who love God, to those who are **called** according to *His* purpose. For those whom He foreknew, He also **predestined** *to become* conformed to the image of His Son, so that He would be the firstborn among many brethren; and these whom He **predestined**, He also **called**; and these whom He **called**, He also justified; and these whom He justified, He also glorified.
>
> —Romans 8:28-30
> (emphasis added via boldface)

> So then He has mercy on whom He desires, and He hardens whom He desires. You will say to me then, "Why does He still find fault? For who resists His will?" On the contrary, who are you, O man, who answers back to God? The thing molded will not say to the

molder, "Why did you make me like this," will it? Or does not the potter have a right over the clay, to make from the same lump one vessel for honorable use and another for common use? What if God, although willing to demonstrate His wrath and to make His power known, endured with much patience vessels of wrath **prepared for destruction**? And *He did so* to make known the riches of His glory upon vessels of mercy, which He **prepared beforehand for glory**, *even* us, whom He also called, not from among Jews only, but also from among Gentiles.

—Romans 9:18-24

(emphasis added via boldface)[91]

However, in Romans, Paul's point is a little different than in Ephesians. First, notice that juxtaposed with these statements supporting predestination is the ultimate expression of free will: "to those who love God." (Romans 8:28)[92] Love is nothing if not freely given. Furthermore, throughout Romans, Paul emphasizes the importance of faith,[93] which presents us with the choice of following God or pursuing our own agenda. If Paul, one of the most articulate letter writers in history, truly meant that everyone's eternal fate is predetermined, he would have clearly said so. But that is not what he meant, for *when Paul talks of predestination in Romans, he is speaking primarily of a people, not individuals.*

The Jews were God's "chosen" people (Deuteronomy 7:6),[94] "entrusted with the oracles of God" (Romans 3:2). The Lord chose Abraham.[95] The Lord chose Isaac instead of Ishmael,[96] Jacob rather than Esau.[97] The Lord later rejected the ten tribes (i.e., the descendants of nine of Jacob's twelve sons[98]), because of their unfaithfulness, ultimately allowing them to be carried into exile, dispersed, and lost to history.[99] Many times in the Old Testament, the Lord rejected *individuals*, often due to their unfaithfulness, but he never rejected his "chosen" people. In Romans, Paul seeks to demonstrate that God has now chosen a new people—Christians.[100]

Paul begins by arguing that the reliance of the Jewish people upon their special relationship with God as his "chosen" people, or upon the Law that God entrusted to them,[101] will not save them. Thus, Paul points out that everyone—Jew and Gentile alike—falls short of what the Law requires,[102] and that those Jews who disobey God's Law will suffer God's judgment despite their special status.[103] Therefore, both Jew and Gentile must rely on faith in Christ for salvation, rather than depending on the Law or their own righteousness.[104] Even if we want to comply with the Law's requirements, we cannot actually do it.[105]

In later chapters of Romans, Paul anticipates the objection that the substitution of the Christians for the Jews as God's "chosen" people would violate his promise to Abraham. Not so, responds Paul, for many of the Christians whom God has chosen are Jews, like Paul.[106] God's promise to Abraham does not fail merely because he moves forward with some, rather than all, of Abraham's descendants—which is exactly what he did in Abraham's day, when he chose the descendants of Isaac rather than those of Ishmael.[107]

Thus, God chose some of the Jews and Gentiles of Paul's day—including Paul himself—to see, hear, and understand God's new message of salvation through faith in

Christ. And if some were chosen, obviously others were not. Is this predestination? Of course. But it is not universal pre-destination—the idea that God has predetermined every-one's eternal fate—a fact Paul implicitly recognizes when he expresses hope and confidence that many of his fellow Jews may yet be saved through faith in Christ.[108]

This is the context of the "predestination" verses in chapters 8 and 9 of Romans, which are part of Paul's argu-ment. He is saying that God has predestined some to become Christians in order to accomplish his purpose, which is to build up a people who will seek salvation through a loving, trusting relationship with Christ, rather than through their own merit and efforts. This does not mean that all others are condemned,[109] but only that they were not granted the spe-cial privilege of being "chosen." If this nevertheless seems unfair, since some receive this privilege and others do not, Paul has a response: "who are you, O man, who answers back to God?" (Romans 9:20) And by the way, Paul—and many others—paid a heavy price for this special privilege.[110]

The Toughest Nuts to Crack

Lastly, we come to a few verses that initially seem ir-reconcilable with the idea of free will, because they appear to speak of individuals being predestined for eternal condem-nation (in each case, I have used boldface to emphasize the relevant language):

> *Jude 4*: For certain persons have crept in unno-ticed, **those who were long beforehand marked out for this condemnation**, ungodly persons who turn the grace of our God into li-

centiousness and deny our only Master and Lord, Jesus Christ.

Romans 9:22: What if God, although willing to demonstrate His wrath and to make His power known, endured with much patience vessels of wrath **prepared for destruction**?

Revelation 13:8: All who dwell on the earth will worship him, *everyone* **whose name has not been written from the foundation of the world in the book of life** of the Lamb who has been slain.[111]

Revelation 17:8 (An angel speaking): "The beast that you saw was, and is not, and is about to come up out of the abyss and go to destruction. And those who dwell on the earth, **whose name has not been written in the book of life from the foundation of the world**, will wonder when they see the beast, that he was and is not and will come."

First, we must not read more into these verses than is there. For example, the author of Jude does not explicitly say that he is referring to *eternal* condemnation. Yet even if we assume that much, the Greek word, *palai*, simply means "long ago," without specifying how long ago. Jesus uses the same word in Matthew 11:21, when he says:

> "Woe to you, Chorazin! Woe to you, Bethsaida! For if the miracles had occurred in Tyre and Sidon which occurred in you, they would have repented long ago in sackcloth and ashes."[112]

Peter also uses the word, which in the following verse is simply translated as "former": "For he who lacks these *qualities* is blind *or* short-sighted, having forgotten *his* purification from his former sins." (2 Peter 1:9)

So the author of Jude is not saying that these "ungodly persons" were predestined for condemnation from birth. Perhaps they were instead "marked out for this condemnation" as a result of a decision to reject God and embrace wickedness. In addition, Jude does not say that these persons are beyond redemption.

Turning next to Romans 9:22, we have already discussed the general context of this verse, which is God's choice of the Christians (including Jewish Christians), in place of the Jews, to carry forward his new message of redemption. In Chapter Nine, Paul talks about God's choice of Isaac over Ishmael, Jacob over Esau, and God's hardening of Pharaoh's heart. None of these Old Testament references has anything to do with eternal salvation. Instead, Paul is talking about God's use of people to carry out his purposes in this life and in this world.

Thus, when Paul talks about vessels prepared for "destruction" in Romans 9:22, the context suggests that he is *not* talking about eternal condemnation. Perhaps he means that these people are destroying their own lives by rejecting God, or maybe he is prophetically referring to the destruction of Jerusalem and the dispersal of the Jews by the Romans in 70 A.D. While both are possibilities, I believe Paul is using a metaphor to describe God's replacement of the Jews with the Christians as his ambassadors in this life. In other words, the Jewish people's special standing with God has in a sense been destroyed. Such an interpretation would be consistent with the context of both Chapter Nine and Romans in general.

Before we leave Romans 9:22, I must also point out the contrast between that verse and Romans 9:23. In the latter, God is the One who prepares "vessels of mercy" for glory. Romans 9:22 is different. It refers to "vessels of wrath prepared for destruction," without specifying who prepared them. *If* these verses do in fact refer to the eternal fate of individuals, then this difference means that someone other than God could be responsible for the destiny of the vessels of wrath. Perhaps they prepared themselves for their fate through their rejection of God and his Christ.

What about Revelation 13:8 and 17:8? At first glance, these two verses appear to state the strongest case for predestination in the entire Bible—at least with regard to eternal salvation.[113] This is especially so when we consider them in combination with Revelation 20:15, which says: "And if anyone's name was not found written in the book of life, he was thrown into the lake of fire." Since having your name in the "book of life" symbolizes salvation, the author of Revelation[114] seems to be saying that a person's eternal salvation (or condemnation) has been decided "from the foundation of the world." But for many reasons, this interpretation is wrong.

First, keep in mind that Revelation 13:8 and 17:8 do not themselves say that those "whose name has not been written from the foundation of the world in the book of life" are eternally condemned, but only that they will worship and marvel at the wicked "beast." Perhaps God will save some, or many, in the end. Revelation 20:15 does not say otherwise, for while it says that those whose names are not in the "book of life" are thrown into the lake of fire, the phrase "from the foundation of the world" is conspicuously absent. This omission is critical, because other verses demonstrate that the names written in this "book of life" can *change*.

One such verse is Revelation 3:5, which implies that names in the "book of life" can be erased from it:

> [Jesus speaking] He who overcomes will thus be clothed in white garments; and I will not erase his name from the book of life, and I will confess his name before My Father and before His angels.

Psalm 69:28 implies the same:

> May they be blotted out of the book of life
> And may they not be recorded with the righteous.

If names can be deleted from the "book of life," perhaps names can be added, too. Let's see what else Revelation says about this "book of life" (in this quote, John is speaking about the New Jerusalem):

> In the daytime (for there will be no night there) its gates will never be closed; and they will bring the glory and the honor of the nations into it; and nothing unclean, and no one who practices abomination and lying, shall ever come into it, but only those whose names are written in the Lamb's book of life.
> —Revelation 21:25-27[115]

In this passage, "those whose names are written in the Lamb's book of life" are those who are morally "clean" and do not practice "abomination and lying"—in other words, those whom God has purified from sin. This is reminiscent of Revelation 3:5, quoted above, in which he who "overcomes" is clothed in white—also symbolic of purification—and is not erased from the book of life. In Revelation 3:5, this purification results, at least in part, from deliberate, persistent action (overcoming), rather than divine selection. The author of Revelation uses this word, "overcomes," frequently.[116]

How do we overcome and thus remain in the book of life? The First Letter of John says we do so through our *pisteuô*-faith:

> For whatever is born of God overcomes the world; and this is the victory that has overcome the world—our faith. Who is the one who overcomes the world, but he who believes that Jesus is the Son of God?
>
> —1 John 5:4-5

Thus, Revelation 13:8 and 17:8 do not truly say that our eternal destiny is fixed from birth. They merely say that the worshipers of the beast will be those whose names are not in the book of life.[117] The support these verses initially appear to offer for the doctrine of predestination evaporates in the light of Revelation's simultaneous insistence that people's actions and choices are critical to their salvation.

Furthermore, Revelation (like all of the New Testament books) contains many verses which make sense only if people have free will, such as those emphasizing repentance,[118] faith,[119] love,[120] and perseverance,[121] and those which encourage or warn the reader about the consequences of certain actions.[122] In the end, Revelation confirms that our eternal fate rests, at least in part, on our decisions and choices.

Beyond Shallow Faith

On the other hand, if we interpret Revelation 13:8 and 17:8 to mean that everyone's eternal destiny has been unalterably fixed from time immemorial, then we annul most of the New Testament, including Jesus' talk about the importance of love, Paul's calls to embrace faith, and large parts of Revelation itself. After all, why would the biblical writers urge me to repent if I'm doomed—or saved—regardless of what I decide to do? That would be like telling me how to win a game that is already over.

Then what are Revelation 13:8 and 17:8 really trying to say? Both describe events which take place in the end times, so they probably have a meaning similar to Ephesians 1:3-13. In other words, a few in those last days will be predestined for salvation—i.e., those whose names are written in the book of life—while everyone else will worship the wicked "beast," leaving their eternal destiny unresolved.

Conclusion. What can we conclude? First, God has indeed predestined us in many ways. Our genetic structure, the time and place of our birth, the quality and circumstances of our family, our innate talents and abilities, and many other factors beyond our control all conspire to make us what we become. As a result, our freedom in this life may be much more limited and illusory than many of us imagine.

Furthermore, the New Testament teaches that every one of us is, in a sense, predestined for condemnation, because none of us is good enough to *earn* our way into Heaven ("for all have sinned and fall short of the glory of God," Romans 3:23). We are like criminals condemned to die ("the wages of sin is death," Romans 6:23). Even those who *want* to be good find, when they are honest with themselves, that they come up short: "For the good that I want, I do not do, but I practice the very evil that I do not want." (Romans 7:19) Jesus and Paul refer to this as slavery to sin.[123] Because of our slavery to sin we cannot please God[124]—salvation is beyond our reach.

But God can save us. He takes the initiative; we merely respond. And that is where freedom enters the picture, for the New Testament teaches that God will save those who *choose* to be in relationship with him.[125] While I do not doubt that God has the power to deny us that choice, he limits himself in order to give us a truly free choice.

Perhaps 1 John 4:19 best summarizes this delicate balance in the New Testament between free will and predestination: "We love, because He first loved us." We certainly have much less freedom than we imagine, but God, at a minimum, allows each of us the freedom to choose whether or not to commit ourselves to him.[126] And our eternal destiny depends on that choice.[127]

Endnotes for Chapter Ten, "Is Free Will an Illusion?"

1. As Jesus pointed out: "which of you by worrying can add a *single* hour to his life's span?" (Luke 12:25)

2. The story of my conversion to Christianity does not follow this pattern. I was an agnostic who committed my life to Christ as a young adult.

3. I do not subscribe to the traditional view of Hell as fire, brimstone, and eternal torture, nor do I believe that Scripture supports such a view. For a discussion of what Scripture truly says about Hell, see Chapter Five of my book, *Beyond Blind Faith*, entitled "What Hell Is Really Like."

4. St. Augustine lived from 354 to 430 A.D.

5. John Calvin (1509 - 1564) and John Knox (ca. 1505 - 1572) were two of the leaders of the Protestant Reformation, along with Martin Luther and others.

6. See for example: Matthew 4:19, 8:22, 9:9, 19:21; Mark 1:17, 2:14, 10:21; Luke 5:27, 9:59, 18:22; John 1:43, 21:19, 21:22.

7. See Matthew 19:16-22, Mark 10:17-22, and Luke 18:18-23.

8. For example, see Mark 1:44: "go, show yourself to the priest." See also: Matthew 19:21, 28:7,28:10, 28:19-20; Mark 2:11, 5:19, 11:2, 14:13, 16:7; Luke 5:14, 7:22, 8:38-39, 13:32, 19:30, 22:8; John 4:16, 4:50, 7:8, 9:7, 20:17; Acts 9:11, 9:15, 22:10, 22:18, 22:21.

9. For example, Luke 6:8 says: "He said to the man with the withered hand, 'Get up and come forward!' " Or John 2:7-8: "Jesus said to them, 'Fill the waterpots with water.' So they filled them up to the brim. And He said to them, 'Draw *some* out now and take it to the headwaiter.' So they took it *to him*." See also: Matthew 16:20; Mark 3:5, 6:10-11, 7:36, 8:26, 9:9, 9:39, 10:14, 11:1-3, 14:13-16; Luke 5:3-4, 6:10, 9:50, 10:2-12, 19:5, 19:30-31, 20:24, 22:19, 22:40, 22:46, 24:39, 24:49; John 1:39, 2:16, 4:7, 5:8, 5:14, 6:12, 11:39, 11:44, 12:7, 18:11, 21:6, 21:10, 21:12; Acts 1:4.

10. Mark 7:36 says: "And He gave them orders not to tell anyone; but the more He ordered them, the more widely they continued to proclaim it." Other examples of people not doing what Jesus told them to do include Mark 1:44-45 and 6:11, and Luke 10:10-12.

11. See Mark 6:1-6 and Matthew 13:54-58.

12. For example, see Matthew 20:25-28:

> But Jesus called them to Himself and said, "You know that the rulers of the Gentiles lord it over them, and *their* great men exercise authority over them. It is not this way among you, but whoever wishes to become great among you shall be your servant, and whoever wishes to be first among you shall be your slave; just as the Son of Man did not come to be served, but to serve, and to give His life a ransom for many."

See also, Matthew 18:1-6, 18:10; Mark 9:35-37, 10:15; Luke 9:48, 14:8-11, 18:13-14, 18:16-17, 22:26, 13:14-15.

13. Matthew 7:1-5; Luke 6:37, 6:41-42

14. Matthew 6:14-15, 18:34-35; Luke 6:27-29

15. Matthew 5:32; Mark 10:2-12; Luke 16:18

16. Matthew 6:19-20, 16:24-27, 22:21; Mark 8:34-38, 12:17; Luke 9:23-26, 9:61-62, 11:28, 12:15, 12:22-23, 12:33-34, 14:26-27, 14:33, 16:9, 20:25, 21:34

17. See Matthew 5:44-47; Luke 6:27-38, 10:25-37, 14:12-14; John 13:34-35, 15:12, 15:17; and see Luke 3:10-14, where John the Baptist preaches a similar message.

18. See Matthew 5:19-20, 12:33-37, 15:18-20, 18:8-9, 23:1-3, 23:25-28; Mark 7:20-23, 9:43-48, 10:19; Luke 11:39-42, 18:20; John 5:28-29, 7:19, 8:11, 8:39; see also, Matthew 3:8 and Luke 3:8, where John the Baptist delivers a similar message.

19. For example, in John 14:23-24, Jesus says:

> If anyone loves Me, he will keep My word; and My Father will love him, and We will come to him and make Our abode with him. He who does not love Me does not keep My words; and the word which you hear is not Mine, but the Father's who sent Me.

See also: Matthew 7:21, 10:40-42, 18:7, 19:12, 23:23-24, 25:32-46; Mark 3:28-30, 3:35, 7:6-13, 9:41-42, 9:50, 13:33-37, 14:7; Luke 6:46-49, 8:18, 8:21, 11:9-13, 11:46, 11:52, 12:56-57, 13:23-24, 17:1-2, 17:23, 21:8, 21:36; John 7:24, 8:51, 9:41, 13:17, 14:15, 14:21, 15:10, 15:14, 15:22, 15:24.

20. See also Acts 15:19-20.

Beyond Shallow Faith

21. See also Romans 2:21-23, 6:1-2, 6:12-13, 6:15, 6:19, 12:1-2, and 13:12-14.

22. Romans 2:1,14:1-3, 14:10, 14:13; 1 Corinthians 4:5; James 4:11

23. Romans 12:3, 12:16; 1 Corinthians 3:18; Ephesians 4:2; Philippians 2:3; Colossians 3:12; James 1:21; 1 Peter 3:8, 5:5-6

24. Romans 12:14, 12:17-21, 10:24, 10:32-33, 15:1-2; 2 Corinthians 2:7-8; Galatians 6:1, 6:9-10; Ephesians 4:32; Philippians 2:4; Colossians 3:12-13; 1 Thessalonians 5:15; 2 Timothy 2:24-26; Titus 3:2; 1 Peter 3:8-9; 2 Peter 1:7

25. Acts 24:25; 1 Corinthians 5:9-13, 6:15, 6:18, 9:24-27, 10:8, 15:33-34; 2 Corinthians 7:1, 13:7; Galatians 5:13, 5:16, 5:19-21; Ephesians 4:17-19, 4:22-24, 4:25-31, 5:3-4, 5:7-11; Philippians 2:14-15, 4:8; Colossians 3:5-9; 1 Thessalonians 5:22; 2 Thessalonians 3:6; 1 Timothy 3:8, 3:11, 4:7, 6:9-11; 2 Timothy 2:19, 2:22; Titus 2:11-12; 1 Peter 1:14-15, 2:11-12, 2:16, 4:15; 2 Peter 1:5-6; 3 John 11

26. 1 Corinthians 7:10-13, 7:27

27. Romans 13:1-7; 1 Corinthians 16:15-16; Ephesians 6:1, 6:5; Colossians 3:20, 3:22; 1 Thessalonians 5:12-13; 1 Timothy 6:1-2; Titus 2:9-10, 3:1; Hebrews 13:17; 1 Peter 2:13-15, 2:17-20

28. Romans 14:15, 14:21, 15:7; 1 Corinthians 1:10, 6:4-8; 2 Corinthians 13:11; Galatians 5:15, 5:25-26, 6:2; Ephesians 4:1-3, 5:2, 5:25, 5:33, 6:4, 6:9; Philippians 1:27, 2:2; Colossians 3:14, 3:19, 4:1; 1 Thessalonians 4:9, 5:13; 1 Timothy 6:17-18; 2 Timothy 2:23-24; Titus 3:9-10; Hebrews 12:14-15; James 2:8; 1 Peter 1:22, 2:17, 4:8-9; 1 John 3:11, 3:16-18, 3:23, 4:7-8, 4:11-12, 4:21; 2 John 5

29. For example: Acts 10:13-15, 17:29; Romans 6:16, 14:5, 14:20, 16:17-19; 1 Corinthians 3:10, 3:21, 4:6, 4:16-17, 6:9-10, 7:5, 7:9, 7:15, 7:17-20, 7:21-24, 7:36, 7:38-40, 8:9, 10:7, 10:9-10, 10:14, 10:25-29, 11:1, 11:27-28, 11:33-34, 12:31, 14:1, 14:12-13, 14:27-32, 14:34-35, 14:39-40; 2 Corinthians 6:14, 9:7; Galatians 4:12, 6:6-8; Ephesians 5:15, 5:17-22, 6:7, 6:18; Philippians 2:5, 4:6, 4:9; Colossians 3:15-18, 3:21, 3:23, 4:2, 4:5-6; 1 Thessalonians 2:11-12, 4:1, 4:10-11, 5:14, 5:16-21; 2 Thessalonians 3:11-15; 1 Timothy 2:8-11, 4:12, 5:1-3, 5:8, 5:16, 6:13-14; 2 Timothy 2:14, 2:16; Titus 2:1-4, 2:6-7, 3:8, 3:14; Hebrews 10:24-25, 12:1, 12:12-13, 13:2-5, 13:15-16; James 1:9-10, 1:19, 1:22-27, 2:1-4, 2:9, 3:10, 3:13-14, 4:15, 5:7-9, 5:12-14, 5:16; 1 Peter 2:1-2, 3:1, 3:7, 4:7, 4:16; 1 John 2:3-4, 2:15, 5:3, 5:21; 2 John 6; 3 John 5-8; Jude 22-23.

30. See also Mark 1:14-15.

31. See also Matthew 3:1-2 and Luke 3:2-3.

32. See Acts 2:37-38:

> Now when they heard *this*, they were pierced to the heart, and said to Peter and the rest of the apostles, "Brethren, what shall we do?" Peter *said* to them, "Repent, and each of you be baptized in the name of Jesus Christ for the forgiveness of your sins; and you will receive the gift of the Holy Spirit."

33. See Matthew 11:21, 12:41-42; Mark 6:12; Luke 5:31-32, Luke 10:13, 11:32, 13:2-5, 15:7, 15:10, 16:30, Luke 17:3-4, 24:47; Acts 3:19, 8:22, 11:18, 17:30, 19:4, 20:21, 26:19-20; Romans 2:5; 2 Corinthians 7:9-10, 12:21; 2 Timothy 2:24-26; Hebrews 6:4-6; 2 Peter 3:9; Revelation 2:4-5, 2:16, 2:20-22, 3:3, 3:19, 9:20-21; see also Mark 2:17, which is similar to Luke 5:31-32.

34. *Webster's* defines "repent" as:

> 1. to feel sorry or self-reproachful for what one has done or failed to do; be conscience-stricken or contrite (often with *of*) 2. to feel such regret or dissatisfaction over some past action, intention, etc. as to change one's mind about (often with *of*) [to *repent* of one's generosity] 3. to feel so contrite over one's sins as to change, or decide to change, one's ways; be penitent.

Guralnik, *Webster's New World Dictionary of the American Language*.

35. See also Matthew 22:36-40 and Luke 10:25-28. In the quotation, Jesus quotes Deuteronomy 6:4-5 and Leviticus 19:18.

36. When you see the English word "love" in the New Testament, the original Greek is always either *agapaô* (or a derivation thereof) or *phileô* (or a derivation thereof).The latter refers to brotherly love (as in Philadelphia, "City of Brotherly Love"), and is used in the following verses: Matthew 6:5, 10:37, 23:6; Luke 20:46; John 5:20, 11:3, 11:36, 12:25, 15:19, 16:27, 20:2, 21:15-17; Romans 12:10; 1 Corinthians 16:22; 1 Thessalonians 4:9; 1 Timothy 3:3, 6:10; Titus 2:4, 3:4, 3:15; Hebrews 13:1, 13:5; 1 Peter 1:22; 3 John 1:9; Revelation 3:19, 22:15.

Beyond Shallow Faith

Agapaô is used much more frequently than *phileô* in the New Testament: Matthew 5:43-44, 5:46, 6:24, 19:19, 22:37, 22:39, 24:12; Mark 10:21, 12:30-31, 12:33; Luke 6:27, 6:32, 6:35, 7:5, 7:42, 7:47, 10:27, 11:42-43, 16:13; John 3:16, 3:19, 3:35, 5:42, 8:42, 10:17, 11:5, 12:43, 13:1, 13:23, 13:34-35, 14:15, 14:21, 14:23-24, 14:28, 14:31, 15:9-10, 15:12-13, 15:17, 17:23-24, 17:26, 19:26, 21:7, 21:15-16, 21:20; Romans 5:5, 5:8, 8:28, 8:35, 8:37, 8:39, 9:13, 12:9, 13:8-10, 14:15, 15:30; 1 Corinthians 2:9, 4:21, 8:1, 8:3, 13:1-4, 13:8, 13:13, 14:1, 16:14, 16:24; 2 Corinthians 2:4, 2:8, 5:14, 6:6, 8:7-8, 8:24, 9:7, 11:11, 12:15, 13:11, 13:14; Galatians 2:20, 5:6, 5:13-14, 5:22; Ephesians 1:4, 1:15, 2:4, 3:17, 3:19, 4:2, 4:15-16, 5:2, 5:25, 5:28, 5:33, 6:23, 6:35; Philippians 1:9, 1:16, 2:1-2; Colossians 1:4, 1:8, 2:2, 3:14, 3:19; 1 Thessalonians 1:3, 3:6, 3:12, 4:9, 5:8, 5:13; 2 Thessalonians 1:3, 2:10, 2:16, 3:5; 1 Timothy 1:5, 1:14, 2:15, 4:12, 6:11; 2 Timothy 1:7, 1:13, 2:22, 3:10, 4:8, 4:10; Titus 2:2; Philemon 1:5, 1:7; Hebrews 1:9, 6:10, 10:24, 12:6; James 1:12, 2:5, 2:8; 1 Peter 1:8, 1:22, 2:17, 3:10, 4:8, 5:14; 2 Peter 1:7, 2:15; 1 John 2:5, 2:10, 2:15, 3:1, 3:10-11, 3:14, 3:16-18, 3:23, 4:7-12, 4:16-21, 5:1-3; 2 John 1:1, 1:3, 1:5-6; 3 John 1:1, 1:6; Jude 1:2, 1:12, 1:21; Revelation 1:5, 2:4, 2:19, 3:9, 12:11.

Both *agapaô* and *phileô* are used in a few verses: John 21:15-16; 1 Thessalonians 4:9; 1 Peter 1:22.

37. See also Luke 6:27 and 6:35. Paul makes the same point in Romans 12:17-21 (quoting Deuteronomy 32:35 and Proverbs 25:21-22):

> Never pay back evil for evil to anyone. Respect what is right in the sight of all men. If possible, so far as it depends on you, be at peace with all men. Never take your own revenge, beloved, but leave room for the wrath *of God*, for it is written, "VENGEANCE IS MINE, I WILL REPAY," says the Lord. "BUT IF YOUR ENEMY IS HUNGRY, FEED HIM, AND IF HE IS THIRSTY, GIVE HIM A DRINK; FOR IN SO DOING YOU WILL HEAP BURNING COALS ON HIS HEAD." Do not be overcome by evil, but overcome evil with good.

38. See also Luke 14:26-27.

39. See Matthew 5:31-32, 15:3-6, 19:3-9; Mark 7:9-13, 10:2-9; John 19:26-27.

40. See Luke 16:13 (Jesus speaking):

> No servant can serve two masters; for either he will hate the one and love the other, or else he will be devoted to one and despise the other. You cannot serve God and wealth.

See also Matthew 6:24.

41. See also Matthew 9:2-7, 9:22; Mark 2:5-12; Luke 5:20-25, 17:19, 18:42.

42. See also, Luke 5:20. In Matthew 9:22, Mark 5:34, and Luke 17:19 and 18:42, what Jesus literally says is, "Your faith has **saved** you." (Emphasis added via boldface.)

43. Hebrews 11:6

44. "Justification" means that God pronounces us righteous and acquits us of our wrongdoing. See, for example, *The Wycliffe Bible Commentary*, p. 1192 (Romans 3:24), and *Interpreter's Concise Commentary*, p. 127 (Romans 3:24).

45. See Romans 1:16-17, 3:21-22, 3:26, 3:28, 5:1, 9:30-32, 11:20; Galatians 2:16, 3:8, 3:24; Philippians 3:9; 2 Timothy 3:15.

46. Romans 4:1-5, 4:9, 4:13, 4:16-22; Galatians 3:6-7

47. See also Romans 5:2 and Galatians 5:4-6.

48. See also: Acts 15:9, 24:24, 26:18; Romans 1:5, 16:26; 1 Corinthians 2:4-5, 15:14, 15:17, 16:13; 2 Corinthians 1:24, 5:7; Galatians 2:20, 3:2, 3:5, 3:9, 3:14, 3:22-26; Ephesians 3:11-12, 3:17; Philippians 1:27; Colossians 1:3-4, 1:21-23, 2:5-7; 1 Thessalonians 3:5-8, 5:8; 2 Thessalonians 1:3-4, 3:1-2; 1 Timothy 1:3-5, 1:18-19, 2:15, 3:13, 4:12, 6:11-12, 6:20-21; 2 Timothy 1:5, 1:13, 4:7-8; Philemon 4-5; Hebrews 4:2, 6:12, 10:22, 10:39, 11:39-40, 13:7; James 1:5-6; 1 Peter 1:8-9; 2 Peter 1:5; 1 John 5:4; Jude 20-21; Revelation 2:10, 14:12.

49. The New Testament contains many other references to the importance of belief. See, for example: Matthew 21:31-32; Mark 1:15; Luke 12:46, 24:25; John 1:7, 1:12, 3:18, 3:36, 5:24, 5:38, 5:44-47, 6:29, 6:35-36, 6:40, 6:47, 7:37-38, 8:24, 8:31-32, 9:35, 11:25-26, 11:40, 11:42, 12:36, 12:44, 12:46, 14:1, 14:11, 17:20, 19:35, 20:27-29, 20:31; Acts 10:43, 13:39, 16:31, 19:4; Romans 3:21-22, 4:16-20, 4:23-24, 10:4, 10:8-11, 10:14, 11:20, 11:23; 1 Corinthians 1:21, 3:5, 15:2, 15:11; Galatians 2:16, 3:6, 3:22; Ephesians 1:13, 1:18-19; 1 Thessalonians 2:13; 2 Thessalonians 1:10, 2:12; 1 Timothy

1:16, 4:10, 4:12; Hebrews 3:12, 3:19, 4:3, 11:6; 1 Peter 1:8, 2:6-7; 1 John 3:23, 5:10-11, 5:13.

50. For more on this topic, see my book, *Beyond Blind Faith*, Chapter Four, "For God So Loved . . . Well, Wait a Minute."

51. Matthew 10:32-33; Luke 12:8-9; Romans 10:9-10; 1 Timothy 6:12; James 5:16; 1 John 1:9, 2:23, 4:15

52. Matthew 10:22, 24:13; Luke 21:19; Acts 11:23; 2 Timothy 2:12; 1 Corinthians 10:13; 2 Timothy 4:5; Hebrews 10:36, 12:7; James 1:12; 1 Peter 2:20. Many other verses speak in similar terms, such as the need to "stand firm," "hold fast," or to "continue in the faith," and the need for "perseverance." For example, see Luke 22:28-30; Acts 14:22; Romans 2:7, 8:25; 11:22; 1 Corinthians 15:2, 15:58, 16:13; Philippians 4:1; 2 Thessalonians 1:4, 2:15; 1 Timothy 4:16, 6:11; Titus 1:9; Hebrews 3:6, 3:14, 10:23; 2 Peter 1:6; Revelation 14:12.

53. Matthew 6:14-15, 18:21-22, 18:35; Mark 11:25; Luke 17:3-4; 2 Corinthians 2:7; see also, Matthew 6:12 and Luke 11:4.

54. Matthew 7:21-23; Luke 6:46; John 3:36; Acts 5:29, 5:32; Romans 6:12-19; 2 Thessalonians 3:14; Hebrews 5:9

55. See also Luke 1:30-33, 2:10-11, 2:25-34; John 17:24, 18:37.

56. See also Matthew 12:40, 16:21, 17:9, 17:12, 17:22-23, 20:17-19, 20:22, 26:39, 26:42, 27:63; Mark 8:31, 10:32-34, 14:35-36; Luke 9:21-22, 9:43-44, 13:33, 17:25, 18:31-33, 22:15, 22:37, 22:42, 24:26, 24:44, 24:46; John 3:14, 7:8, 7:30, 7:33, 13:1, 13:3, 16:19-22, 16:28, 18:4, 18:11; Acts 2:22-23, 3:18, 4:27-28.

57. John 6:70-71 and Matthew 26:31-35. See also, Matthew 26:21-25; Mark 14:18-21; Luke 22:3-6; John 6:64, 13:2, 13:11, 13:18, 13:21, 13:25-27; Acts 1:16. Of course, Peter *did* deny Jesus three times, and the disciples all deserted him, just as Jesus predicted. See Matthew 26:56 and 26:69-75. The other Gospels tell a similar story: Mark 14:27-31, 14:50, 14:66-72; Luke 22:31-34, 22:54-62; John 13:36-38, 16:32, 18:15-18, 18:25-27.

58. For example, see Galatians 1:15-17 (emphasis supplied via boldface):

> But when God, **who had set me apart *even* from my mother's womb and called me through His grace, was pleased to reveal His Son in me so that I might preach Him among the Gentiles**, I did not immediately consult

with flesh and blood, nor did I go up to Jerusalem to those who were apostles before me; but I went away to Arabia, and returned once more to Damascus.

See also Acts 9:15-16, 22:10; Romans 1:1-2, 15:15-16; 1 Corinthians 15:10; 2 Corinthians 1:1, 10:8, 13:10; Galatians 1:1; Colossians 1:1, 1:25; 2 Timothy 1:11.

59. Acts 9:3-8, 9:15-16, 26:12-18

60. Acts 23:11, 27:23-24

61. See, for example, Acts 13:2-4, 16:6-10, 20:22-23, 21:10-14, 22:14-15; 1 Corinthians 9:16-17; 2 Corinthians 2:12-13; 1 Thessalonians 3:3-4.

62. Luke 1:13-17; John 1:6-7; and see Matthew 11:9-10.

63. John 11:1-44

64. John 19:10-11

65. John 15:16, 15:19, 16:2, 21:18-19; Acts 1:7-8, 15:7

66. Acts 9:3-18; see also 2 Corinthians 12:2-4.

67. John 20:24-29

68. Acts 13:6-12

69. See 1 Thessalonians 1:4-5, which is quoted on page 103.

70. See also Romans 9:10-13.

71. Personally, I believe God knew what Pharaoh would do because he knew what was in Pharaoh's heart. Pharaoh's actions were predestined in the sense that they were predictable. He was going to act in accordance with his nature, as God knew he would.

72. Matthew 22:11-14; Mark 13:20-22, 13:27; Luke 18:7; John 10:3-5, 15:16, 15:19; Acts 1:24-26, 2:39, 10:40-41, 13:48, 15:7, 16:9-10; Romans 1:5-6, 8:28-30, 8:33, 9:10-13, 9:24, 11:4-5. 11:7, 11:28-29; 1 Corinthians 1:1-2, 1:9, 1:24, 1:26-30, 7:17-24; Galatians 1:6, 5:8, 5:13; Ephesians 1:4, 1:18, 4:1, 4:4; Colossians 3:12, 3:15; 1 Thessalonians 1:4, 4:7; 2 Thessalonians 2:13-14; 1 Timothy 6:12; 2 Timothy 1:9, 2:10; Titus 1:1; Hebrews 9:15; James 2:5; 1 Peter 1:1-2, 2:9, 2:21, 3:9, 5:10, 5:13; 2 Peter 1:3, 1:10; 2 John 1, 13; Jude 1; Revelation 17:14

73. Luke 6:13-16; Acts 1:24-26, 15:7, 16:9-10; Romans 9:11

74. I include in the "ambiguous" category both the verses that do not necessarily refer to eternal salvation and those that do not necessarily promise eternal salvation to the "chosen" or "called." See, for example: Matthew 22:14; Mark 13:20-22; Luke 18:7; John 10:3, 15:16, 15:19; Acts 2:39, 10:40-41; Romans 1:5-6, 8:28, 8:33, 9:24, 11:5, 11:7, 11:28-29; 1 Corinthians 1:1-2, 1:9, 1:24, 1:26-30, 7:17-24; Galatians 1:6, 5:8, 5:13; Ephesians 1:18, 4:1, 4:4; Colossians 3:12, 3:15; 1 Thessalonians 1:4, 4:7; 2 Timothy 1:9; Titus 1:1; James 2:5; 1 Peter 1:1-2, 2:9-10, 2:21, 3:9, 5:13; 2 Peter 1:3, 1:10; 2 John 1, 13; Jude 1; Revelation 17:14.

75. And see Mark 13:27; Romans 8:29-30; 1 Timothy 6:12; 2 Timothy 2:10; Hebrews 9:15.

76. Matthew 3:12, 13:24-30, 15:12-14; Luke 3:17

77. Matthew 7:15-20; Luke 6:43-45 (but see also Matthew 12:33, which implies that we have at least some free will in deciding what type of "tree" we will be: "Either make the tree good and its fruit good, or make the tree bad and its fruit bad; for the tree is known by its fruit.")

78. Matthew 13:3-9, 13:18-23; Mark 4:3-9, 4:14-20; Luke 8:5-8, 8:11-15

79. Matthew 11:25, 13:10-15; Mark 4:11-12; Luke 8:9-10, 10:21-22, 19:42; John 10:26-29, 12:37-40. Paul makes a similar point in verses such as: 1 Corinthians 2:14; 2 Corinthians 3:14-16, 4:3-4.

80. John 10:14-16, 10:26-28, and 18:37; and see Matthew 19:11: "But He said to them, 'Not all men *can* accept this statement, but *only* those to whom it has been given.' " See also, 1 John 4:6, where John's message is similar.

81. John 6:37, 6:39, 10:29, 17:1-2, 17:6, 17:9, and 17:24

82. For example, see Matthew 23:34-35; Mark 14:13-16; Luke 11:49-51, 19:42-44, 21:6, 21:9-24, 22:10-13; John 19:23-24; Acts 27:22-24; 2 Timothy 3:1-2, 4:3-4; Revelation 13:8.

83. This idea of God's ultimate control is also reflected in Acts 18:21.

84. See also John 6:65, which is similar. And see Romans 2:4 and 2 Timothy 2:25-26.

85. See Colossians 4:14, where Paul refers to "Luke, the beloved physician." The Gospel of Luke and Acts have similar introductions (Luke 1:1-4, Acts 1:1-2), as well as similar style and vocabulary, which has con-

vinced biblical scholars that a single author wrote both. Early Christian writers identified Luke, a companion of Paul, as the author. Luke's ties to Paul are established by Paul's references to him (Colossians 4:14, 2 Timothy 4:11, Philemon 24), as well as the switch from third person ("they") to first person ("we") in Acts. (Compare Acts 16:6-7 and 16:10.)

86. Acts 22:3; Philippians 3:5

87. For example, see Romans 8:28: "And we know that God causes all things to work together for good to those who love God, to those who are called according to *His* purpose." The phrase, "those who love God," is an expression of free will, without which love is impossible, but "those who are called" implies predestination.

88. I do not ignore the implications of Matthew 26:24, which states: "The Son of Man *is to* go, just as it is written of Him; but woe to that man by whom the Son of Man is betrayed! It would have been good for that man if he had not been born." (See also Mark 14:21 and Luke 22:22.) This verse might refer to Judas' ultimate destiny, but it could just as easily be interpreted as a recognition of the severe guilt, shame, and despair he would feel as he saw Jesus condemned—feelings that led Judas to commit suicide. See Matthew 27:3-5.

89. However, see also 1 Corinthians 9:26-27, where Paul seems to say that he could still lose his salvation:

> Therefore I run in such a way, as not without aim; I box
> in such a way, as not beating the air; but I discipline my
> body and make it my slave, so that, after I have
> preached to others, I myself will not be disqualified.

90. Paul wrote the letter to the Ephesians to Gentiles, which is apparent from Ephesians 2:11, where he addresses his readers as "you, the Gentiles in the flesh, who are called 'Uncircumcision' by the so-called 'Circumcision.' " See also, Ephesians 3:1. Thus, when he says "you," he may specifically have Gentiles in mind. Under this interpretation, the Jews, or at least Jewish Christians, are predestined for salvation, and Gentiles have free will.

91. And see Romans 8:33-34.

92. Similar examples of this type of juxtaposition of free will and predestination appear in other letters, such as 2 Timothy 2:10, where Paul

states: "For this reason I endure all things for the sake of those who are chosen, so that they also may obtain the salvation which is in Christ Jesus *and* with *it* eternal glory." If they are already "chosen" for salvation, why must Paul endure anything to help them obtain it?

93. See, for example, Romans 1:5, 1:8, 1:12, 1:17, 3:22, 3:26-28, 4:5, 4:9, 4:13, 5:1-2, 9:30, 9:32.

94. Deuteronomy 7:6 says: "the LORD your God has chosen you to be a people for His own possession out of all the peoples who are on the face of the earth." See also Deuteronomy 14:2.

95. Genesis 18:19

96. Genesis 17:15-21, 21:12

97. Genesis 25:23

98. The ten tribes were descended from the following nine sons of Israel (Jacob): Reuben, Simeon, Dan, Naphtali, Gad, Asher, Issachar, Zebulun, and Joseph. The tenth tribe came from the fact that Joseph's two sons, Manasseh and Ephraim, each fathered a separate tribe.

99. 2 Kings 15:29, 17:1-23, 18:9-12

100. Peter makes the same point in 1 Peter 2:9-10:

> But you are A CHOSEN RACE, A royal PRIESTHOOD, A HOLY NATION, A PEOPLE FOR *God's* OWN POSSESSION, so that you may proclaim the excellencies of Him who has called you out of darkness into His marvelous light; for you once were NOT A PEOPLE, but now you are THE PEOPLE OF GOD; you had NOT RECEIVED MERCY, but now you have RECEIVED MERCY.

Peter quotes or refers to various Old Testament scriptures in these two verses (indicated by ALL CAPS), including: Isaiah 43:20, Isaiah 61:6, Exodus 19:5-6, Hosea 1:10 and 2:23.

101. The "Law" refers to the Jewish Law, as contained in the first five books of the Old Testament—Genesis, Exodus, Leviticus, Numbers, and Deuteronomy.

102. See Romans 3:9-12, 3:20, 3:23.

103. See Romans 2:3, 2:9, 2:12, 2:17-25.

104. See Romans 1:16-17, 3:21-22, 3:28, 4:3-5, 4:16, 4:22-25.

105. See Romans 7:5, 7:7-25, 8:6-7.

106. See Romans 11:1-5, below (quotes are from 1 Kings 19:10, 19:14, and 19:18):

> I say then, God has not rejected His people, has He? May it never be! For I too am an Israelite, a descendant of Abraham, of the tribe of Benjamin. God has not rejected His people whom He foreknew. Or do you not know what the Scripture says in *the passage about* Elijah, how he pleads with God against Israel? "Lord, THEY HAVE KILLED YOUR PROPHETS, THEY HAVE TORN DOWN YOUR ALTARS, AND I ALONE AM LEFT, AND THEY ARE SEEKING MY LIFE." But what is the divine response to him? "I HAVE KEPT for Myself SEVEN THOUSAND MEN WHO HAVE NOT BOWED THE KNEE TO BAAL." In the same way then, there has also come to be at the present time a remnant according to *God's* gracious choice.

See also, Romans 9:25-28.

107. See Romans 9:6-9, below (quotes are from Genesis 21:12 and Genesis 18:10):

> But *it is* not as though the word of God has failed. For they are not all Israel who are *descended* from Israel; nor are they all children because they are Abraham's descendants, but: "THROUGH ISAAC YOUR DESCENDANTS WILL BE NAMED." That is, it is not the children of the flesh who are children of God, but the children of the promise are regarded as descendants. For this is the word of promise: "AT THIS TIME I WILL COME, AND SARAH SHALL HAVE A SON."

108. See, for example, Romans 11:11-15:

> I say then, they did not stumble so as to fall, did they? May it never be! But by their transgression salvation *has*

> *come* to the Gentiles, to make them jealous. Now if their transgression is riches for the world and their failure is riches for the Gentiles, how much more will their fulfillment be! But I am speaking to you who are Gentiles. Inasmuch then as I am an apostle of Gentiles, I magnify my ministry, if somehow I might move to jealousy my fellow countrymen and save some of them. For if their rejection is the reconciliation of the world, what will *their* acceptance be but life from the dead?

See also, Romans 10:1-3 and 11:23-24.

109. Indeed, in Romans 11:25, Paul refers to a "partial hardening" of Israel, which may imply that God's rejection of the Jews was only temporary.

110. For example, see 2 Corinthians 11:23-27, where Paul recounts his many sufferings for the cause of Christ. He was eventually executed by the Romans in about 64 A.D. as part of the persecution of Christians under Emperor Nero. I discuss the sufferings and deaths of many of Jesus' early followers in Chapter Two of my previous book, *Beyond Blind Faith: Reasons For the Hope We Have (1 Peter 3:15)*, which is entitled: "Is Jesus' Resurrection Fact or Fairy Tale?: The Historical Evidence for the Resurrection of Jesus Christ."

111. Some scholars argue that, in the original Greek, the phrase, "from the foundation of the world," actually modifies "the Lamb who has been slain." Thus, they argue, the verse would more accurately be translated:

> All who dwell on the earth will worship him, *everyone* whose name has not been written in the book of life of the Lamb who has been slain from the foundation of the world.

Even if true, this contention does not explain Revelation 17:8, in which the phrase, "the Lamb who has been slain" is absent.

112. See also Luke 10:13.

113. Psalm 139:16, quoted on page 96.

114. See Revelation 1:4. Tradition says that the John of Revelation 1:4 was John the apostle, the youngest of the Twelve chosen by Jesus, and the

probable author of the Gospel of John and the First Letter of John. He may also have been the author of the Second and Third Letters of John (2 John and 3 John), although that is doubted by many scholars.

115. The "book of life" is also mentioned in Revelation 20:12 and Philippians 4:3. Those verses shed no light for our purposes.

116. See Revelation 2:7, 2:11, 2:17, 2:26, 3:5, 3:12, 3:21, and 21:7.

117. It is possible that those who are alive and whose names *are* recorded in the book of life will have already been raptured—that is, taken to Heaven—by the time the beast is worshiped.

118. See Revelation 2:5, 2:16, 2:21-22, 3:3, 3:19, 9:20-21, 16:9, 16:11.

119. See Revelation 2:19, 13:10, 14:12.

120. See Revelation 2:19.

121. See Revelation 1:9, 2:2-3, 2:19, 13:10, 14:12.

122. See Revelation 1:3: "Blessed is he who reads and those who hear the words of the prophecy, and **heed the things which are written in it**; for the time is near." (Emphasis added via boldface.) Or Revelation 22:18-19, below (emphasis added via boldface):

> I testify to everyone who hears the words of the prophecy of this book: **if anyone adds to them**, God will add to him the plagues which are written in this book; and **if anyone takes away from the words of the book of this prophecy**, God will take away his part from the tree of life and from the holy city, which are written in this book.

123. For example, see John 8:34-36:

> Jesus answered them, "Truly, truly, I say to you, everyone who commits sin is the slave of sin. The slave does not remain in the house forever; the son does remain forever. So if the Son makes you free, you will be free indeed."

And see Romans 6:5-7, 6:15-18, 6:20-23, 7:14; Titus 3:3.

124. See Romans 8:6-8:

Beyond Shallow Faith

> For the mind set on the flesh is death . . . because the mind set on the flesh is hostile toward God; for it does not subject itself to the law of God, for it is not even able *to do so,* and those who are in the flesh cannot please God.

125. I am not saying (as some do) that God cannot or will not save non-Christians. That is a matter best left to God.

126. Indeed, our only choice in this regard may be slavery to sin or slavery to God. See Romans 6:22:

> But now having been freed from sin and enslaved to God, you derive your benefit, resulting in sanctification, and the outcome, eternal life.

127. I do not believe that our opportunity to choose or reject God necessarily ends with our death in this life. Scriptures such as John 5:25, 1 Peter 3:19, and 1 Peter 4:6 seem to say that even those who have died in this world will have at least one more opportunity to accept Christ in the afterlife. For more on this topic, see Chapter Seven of my book, *Beyond Blind Faith*, entitled, "Is Yahweh an Ogre?"

Chapter 11
WHY GOD WON'T SAVE EVERYONE
(Even Though He Would Like To)

Some people believe that God will save everyone—a belief commonly known as "universal salvation."[1] After all, the apostle John wrote that "God is love." (1 John 4:8) Could a loving God really condemn some of his beloved creatures to anything other than Heaven?[2] Numerous Scriptures say he will do so, and regrettably, I believe he *must* do so.

What the Scriptures Say. The New Testament abounds with descriptions of this ultimate judgment and its potentially dire consequences. Jesus spoke of the "narrow gate" that leads to life, contrasting it with the wide way that leads to "destruction." (Matthew 7:13-14)[3] He urged his followers not to fear men, who can only kill the body, but rather to fear God, who can destroy the soul.[4] He described a scene of final judgment, at which some will be condemned because of their hard-heartedness toward their fellow man.[5] Jesus even suggested that drowning or self-mutilation would be preferable to enduring such condemnation.[6]

The apostle Paul warned repeatedly that those who refuse God's free gift of salvation and eternal life will face "death."[7] James 5:19-20 says that anyone who turns a fellow Christian away from sin "will save his soul from death." 2 Peter 3:7 speaks of the "day of judgment and destruction of ungodly men." Many New Testament passages warn of God's wrath and the doom that awaits those who refuse God's mercy, often contrasting their fate with those who receive salvation and eternal life.[8] Many more scriptures foretell God's judgment and/or condemnation.[9]

Paul Was No Fool. In the face of this overwhelming scriptural evidence, those who favor universal salvation point to a few verses that seem to say that God will save *all* people. For example, in John 12:32, Jesus said, "And I, if I am lifted up from the earth, will draw all men to Myself." Paul, in Romans 5:18, said, "So then as through one transgression there resulted condemnation to all men, even so through one act of righteousness there resulted justification of life to all men." And in 1 Corinthians 15:22 he said: "For as in Adam all die, so also in Christ all will be made alive." Can these and similar scriptures[10] be reconciled with the abundant verses that predict judgment, wrath, and condemnation? Yes.[11] Let's begin with Romans 5:18, quoted above.

Three chapters earlier, in Romans 2:3-8, Paul said:

> But do you suppose this, O man, when you pass judgment on those who practice such things and do the same *yourself,* that you will escape the judgment of God? Or do you think lightly of the riches of His kindness and tolerance and patience, not knowing that the kindness of God leads you to repentance? But because of your stubbornness and unrepentant heart you are storing up wrath for yourself in the day of wrath and revelation of the righteous judgment of God, who WILL RENDER TO EACH PERSON ACCORDING TO HIS DEEDS: to those who by perseverance in doing good seek for glory and honor and immortality, eternal life; but to those who are selfishly ambitious and do not obey the truth, but obey unrighteousness, wrath and indignation.[12]

Paul drew a distinction here between those who will receive eternal life and those who will incur God's "wrath and indignation." This passage would be nonsensical if everyone receives eternal life. In Romans 6:21-23, Paul made a similar point:

> Therefore what benefit were you then deriving from the things of which you are now ashamed? For the outcome of those things is death. But now having been freed from sin and enslaved to God, you derive your benefit, resulting in sanctification, and the outcome, eternal life. For the wages of sin is death, but the free gift of God is eternal life in Christ Jesus our Lord.

As in chapter two of Romans, these verses distinguish between those who will receive eternal life and those who will not.

Was Paul so stupid that he would contradict himself within the confines of a single letter? Or do these verses—which talk of judgment, wrath, and death, as contrasted with eternal life—indicate that Paul's meaning in Romans 5:18 is something other than universal salvation? As in any biblical interpretation, context will help us immensely. Let's first look at the historical context.

Like Jesus, most of the earliest Christians were Jews. As Christianity began to spread to Gentiles (i.e., non-Jews),[13] many of these Jewish Christians insisted that the Gentile converts must observe the Jewish Old Testament Law,[14] believing that salvation would come through both Christ and the Law. Paul strongly disagreed, and he wrote Romans (at least in part) to refute the Jewish notion that the Law made them special to God, and that he would save them because of this unique status.[15] Repeatedly in Romans, Paul emphasized that God no longer distinguishes between Jew and Gentile, and that since the Law cannot save the Jews, *all* must rely on faith for salvation.[16] In this context, Paul's reference to "all men" in Romans 5:18 merely highlights his point that Christ did not die merely for the Jews, but for Gentiles as well. In other words, "all men," Jew and Gentile, now have the same chance for salvation through faith in Christ.

Romans 5:17 reinforces this interpretation. That verse says:

> For if by the transgression of the one [Adam],
> death reigned through the one, much more
> those who receive the abundance of grace and
> of the gift of righteousness will reign in life
> through the One, Jesus Christ.

In Romans 5:17-18, Paul contrasted the outcome of Adam's sin, which contaminated all of mankind, with the effect of Jesus' obedience, which reconciled mankind to God and gives us "life" (i.e., eternal life). But in Romans 5:17, Paul does not say that *everyone* receives eternal life, but only "those who receive the abundance of grace and of the gift of righteousness."

Elsewhere in Romans, Paul explains who receives this grace and righteousness—again, not everyone, but instead, those who have faith:

> For we maintain that a man is justified [i.e.,
> made righteous] by faith apart from works of

the Law.

—Romans 3:28

Therefore, having been justified by faith, we have peace with God through our Lord Jesus Christ, through whom also we have obtained our introduction by faith into this grace in which we stand; and we exult in hope of the glory of God.

—Romans 5:1-2

Thus, the scriptural context of Romans 5:18 confirms what the historical context suggests—Paul was not saying that all people will be saved, but that the possibility of eternal salvation is now open to all people, and not merely the Jews. In Paul's theology, those who repent and turn back to God in faith are the ones who will be saved.[17]

John Was No Fool, Either. John 12:32 is another verse cited in support of universal salvation. John 12:32 quotes Jesus as saying, "And I, if I am lifted up from the earth, will draw all men to Myself." But as with Romans 5:18, the verses surrounding John 12:32 compel the conclusion that Jesus did not really mean that *all* people would be saved. Only a few verses earlier, in John 12:25, Jesus stated that some will receive eternal life and some will not: "He who loves his life loses it, and he who hates his life in this world will keep it to life eternal." In the verses that *follow* John 12:32, Jesus warns of the judgment and "darkness" that await those who reject him.[18]

So what is the meaning of John 12:32? Perhaps Jesus, like Paul, simply meant that salvation is now open to all, and not merely the Jews, or perhaps he was pointing out that he was about to die for all men[19]—even for those who would not ultimately receive eternal life. But either way, he did not have universal salvation in mind.

As with Romans 5:18 and John 12:32, each of the verses commonly cited in support of universal salvation can be juxtaposed with verses from the same book that speak of God's judgment, wrath, or condemnation—a strong indication that universal salvation was not the author's original intent:

Universal Salvation	Contrary verses, same book
John 12:32	John 3:18, 3:36, 5:24, 5:28-29,12:25, 12:35, 12:46-48, 15:6
Acts 3:21[20]	Acts 13:46, 17:30-31
Romans 5:18, 11:32	Romans 2:1-9, 2:12, 2:16, 3:5-6, 6:15-16, 6:21-23, 7:5, 8:6-8,8:12-13, 11:21-22, 14:10-12
1 Corinthians 15:22	1 Corinthians 3:16-17, 5:12-13, 11:32
Ephesians 1:10[21]	Ephesians 5:3-6
Colossians 1:20	Colossians 3:5-6, 3:23-25
1 Timothy 2:6	1 Timothy 3:6

Indeed, the advocates of universal salvation must ignore so many contrary Scriptures that they begin to look like wishful thinkers.

Why God Won't Save Everyone. But why should this be so? The Bible says that Jesus Christ died for all of mankind,[22] so God is apparently able to save anyone—or everyone. And I have no doubt that God "desires all men to be saved." (1 Timothy 2:4) If God wants to save everyone, and is able to do so, then why wouldn't he?

Because some of us won't give him that option.

Now I am not so arrogant that I think I know who won't be saved, nor am I trying to tell God whom he should or should not allow into Heaven. But as I discussed in Chapter Two ("Sharing Heaven"), God will require anyone who gets in to leave certain baggage at the door: hatred, bitterness, jealousy, and grudges, for example. Heaven, to truly be Heaven, must be a place of love, kindness, and forgiveness—a place where people no longer seek to inflict physical or emotional pain on each other.[23] A desire to hurt someone, or to see someone hurt, can have no place in Heaven. God will not introduce cancer into a healthy body.

Thus, each of us may face this dilemma at the Judgment Day: forgive and love those we detest, or find ourselves excluded from Eternity. I am confident that we must enter Heaven on God's terms, or not enter it at all. Faced with such a choice, would anyone really cling to their hatred or bitterness, and forego Heaven? Scriptures suggest that many will.

Sincere forgiveness is hard. Unselfish love is even tougher. Can the religious bigot or the racist embrace those they now hate? Will the crime victim be willing to share Heaven with the offender? How about the cuckolded husband or the rejected wife who must forgive their former spouse?

And how about you? Are you able to forgive your enemies? Can you forgive those who have wounded, angered, or offended you most deeply? The answer to this question is likely to have eternal consequences, for Jesus warned us:

> Enter through the narrow gate; for the gate is wide and the way is broad that leads to destruction, and there are many who enter through it. For the gate is small and the way is narrow that leads to life, and there are few who find it.
>
> —Matthew 7:13-14

God will not save everyone, but only those who are willing to enter Heaven through God's "narrow gate" of love and sincere forgiveness. Many will find that path too difficult.[24] I hope that you will not.

Ch. 11 – Why God Won't Save Everyone

Endnotes for Chapter Eleven, "Why God Won't Save Everyone"

1. One of the earliest advocates of this position was the 3rd century Christian writer, Origen.

2. I do not use the word "Hell" because it carries connotations of fire, brimstone, and eternal torture which are not supported by what the New Testament really says about the afterlife. For more on this topic, see Chapter Five of my book, *Beyond Blind Faith: Reasons for the Hope We Have (1 Peter 3:15)*, entitled "What Hell Is Really Like."

3. See also Luke 13:23-28.

4. See Matthew 10:28 and Luke 12:4-5.

5. See Matthew 25:41-46. See also Mark 16:16, although that verse is not contained in the oldest New Testament manuscripts.

6. Matthew 5:29-30, 18:2-9; Mark 9:42-50

7. See Romans 6:15-16, 6:21-23, 7:5, 7:24, 8:6-8, 8:12-13; 2 Corinthians 2:15-16, 4:3-4, 7:10; 2 Thessalonians 2:10-12.

8. See, for example: Luke 3:7-9; John 3:36; Romans 2:1-9, 2:12, 3:5; 1 Corinthians 3:16-17, 11:32; Ephesians 5:3-6; Philippians 1:27-28; Colossians 3:5-6; 1 Thessalonians 5:9; 2 Thessalonians 1:6-9; 1 Timothy 3:2-6; Jude 1:10-13; Revelation 11:16-18, 14:9-11, 20:12-15, 21:5-8.

9. Matthew 7:1-2, 10:14-15, 11:20-24, 12:33-37, 12:41-42; John 3:16-18, 5:24, 5:28-29, 12:47-48; Acts 17:30-31; Romans 2:16, 3:6, 14:10-12; 1 Corinthians 5:12-13; 2 Timothy 4:1; Hebrews 9:27-28, 10:26-31, 12:23, 13:4; James 2:13, 4:12, 5:9, 5:12; 1 Peter 1:17, 4:3-6, 4:17-18; 2 Peter 2:1-10; Jude 1:4-6. See also the following Scriptures, where judgment and condemnation are at least implicit: Matthew 3:7-12, 7:15-19, 8:11-12, 13:36-42, 13:47-50, 18:23-35, 22:1-14, 23:13-14, 24:45-51, 25:26-30; Mark 8:34-38, 12:38-40; Luke 3:17, 6:37-38, 10:13-15, 11:31-32, 12:8-10, 12:42-48, 13:1-5, 16:19-31, 19:27, 20:46-47; John 12:25, 15:6; Acts 13:46; Romans 8:1, 11:13-14, 11:21-22; 1 Corinthians 6:2-3, 9:24-27; Colossians 3:23-25; 1 Thessalonians 5:2-4; Hebrews 2:1-3; 2 Peter 2:12-22, 3:14-17.

10. See Acts 3:21; Romans 11:32; Ephesians 1:10; Colossians 1:20; 1 Timothy 2:6; Titus 2:11; and Hebrews 10:10. I do not include in this list 1 Timothy 2:3-4, which says, "This is good and acceptable in the sight of God our Savior, who desires all men to be saved and to come to the

knowledge of the truth." *Desiring* that all men be saved is far different than *saving* them. (2 Peter 3:9 is similar.)

11. As noted in the Preface, I do not believe that the New Testament writers intended to contradict themselves, or each other. So whenever possible I try to interpret Scripture to avoid or resolve any apparent conflicts, believing this will bring us nearer to the writers' true intent.

12. The phrase in ALL CAPS indicates a quotation from Psalm 62:12 and/or Proverbs 24:12.

13. See, for example, Acts 9:15, 10:1-48, 11:1-18, 13:44-49.

14. The Law, which is primarily derived from the first five books of the Old Testament (Genesis, Exodus, Leviticus, Numbers, and Deuteronomy), not only included the Ten Commandments, but also rules about hygiene, animal sacrifices, feasts and festivals, Temple practices, permitted and prohibited foods, criminal and civil laws, criminal and civil penalties, property rights, etc. And the Law required all males to be circumcised. See Genesis 17:9-14.

15. John the Baptist encountered (and denounced) this belief that God would save the Jews because of their status as descendants of Abraham. For example, see Luke 3:8:

> "Therefore bear fruits in keeping with repentance, and
> do not begin to say to yourselves, 'We have Abraham for
> our father,' for I say to you that from these stones God is
> able to raise up children to Abraham."

See also, Matthew 3:9.

16. See, for example, Romans 1:16, 2:9-11, 2:25-29, 3:9, 3:23, 3:29-30, 9:24, 9:30-32, 10:12.

17. For a fuller discussion of what God wants from us, see Chapter Four of my book, *Beyond Blind Faith*, entitled, "For God So Loved . . . Well, Wait a Minute."

18. See John 12:35 and 12:46-48.

19. The proposition that Jesus Christ died for the sins of all people is a basic precept of Christianity. See, for example, 1 John 2:2: "and He Himself [Christ] is the propitiation for our sins; and not for ours only, but also for *those of* the whole world."

20. Acts 3:21, taken from Peter's speech on Pentecost, merely speaks of the "restoration of all things," which does not necessarily refer to salvation, much less universal salvation.

21. As with Acts 3:21, Ephesians 1:10 is a weak verse to support universal salvation, since it merely refers to "the summing up of all things in Christ."

22. See, for example, 2 Corinthians 5:14-15: "For the love of Christ controls us, having concluded this, that one died for all, therefore all died; and He died for all, so that they who live might no longer live for themselves, but for Him who died and rose again on their behalf." And 1 Timothy 2:6 says that Jesus "gave Himself as a ransom for all."

23. For a discussion of why this is so, see Chapter Two, "Sharing Heaven."

24. I do not foreclose the possibility that God will save some—perhaps many—non-Christians. However, I believe that sincere Christians have a tremendous advantage in this regard because we have been practicing forgiveness in this life, and like anything, we get better at forgiving the more we practice it.

Chapter 12
DID JESUS REALLY HAVE TO DIE?

When I was in college, the followers of Sun Myung Moon told me that Jesus died too soon. His premature death, they claimed, prevented him from establishing the Kingdom of Heaven on earth. So God sent Rev. Moon to accomplish what Jesus failed to do. Rev. Moon is now deceased.[1]

Similarly, a Christian friend of mine insists that Jesus' death must have been a mistake. Surely God would not intentionally inflict such a cruel fate upon anyone, much less his own son.

Jesus' final twenty-four hours before his death were certainly horrific. After going without sleep the night before,[2] He was bound, beaten, spat upon, flogged, mocked, and finally crucified.[3] Crucifixion is a dreadful way to die. The arms are extended and the wrists are nailed to a cross beam, while a single spike is driven through both feet. In this position, breathing becomes labored. To get sufficient oxygen, the unfortunate victim must push upward against the nail in his feet, exacerbating the intense pain. Exhaustion eventually sets in, and the victim dies of asphyxiation. When the Romans needed to speed up death, they would break the victim's legs, thus preventing him from pushing up to get a breath. They did this to the two criminals whom they crucified with Jesus.[4]

So my friend had a point. Crucifixion is one of the most fiendish forms of execution that humankind has ever devised. Yet if we believe the Bible, we must accept two truths that are constant themes in the New Testament: (1) Jesus went to his death willingly and with full knowledge of its cruel nature, and (2) his death was necessary to enable us to have a relationship with God.

Jesus knew and accepted that he must die. Shortly after Peter's confession that Jesus was "the Christ, the Son of the living God" (Matthew 16:16),[5] Jesus broke the news to his disciples that he was going to die. At first, he told them only in vague terms: "From that time Jesus began to show His disciples that He must go to Jerusalem, and suffer many things from the elders and chief priests and scribes, and be killed, and be raised up on the third day." (Matthew 16:21)[6] But as the time grew near, Jesus got more explicit, telling his twelve most devoted followers that

> the Son of Man will be delivered to the chief priests and the scribes; and they will condemn Him to death and will hand Him over to the Gentiles. They will mock Him and spit on Him, and scourge Him and kill *Him*, and three days later He will rise again.
>
> —Mark 10:33-34[7]

Indeed, Matthew and Luke tell us that Jesus specifically predicted that he would be crucified,[8] which was the standard Roman method of execution for non-citizens, especially those convicted of treason—the crime for which Jesus was put to death.[9]

Jesus' words to his disciples the evening before he died[10] once again demonstrate his knowledge of his imminent death. He compared his body to the bread they were eating, and his blood to the wine they drank, adding that his blood would be spilled for them and for many.[11]

The Garden of Gethsemane is where we most clearly see Jesus' *knowledge* of his impending death, as well as his *willingness* to endure it. There he uttered this famous cry of complete obedience to the will of God: "Father, if You are willing, remove this cup from Me; yet not My will, but Yours be done." (Luke 22:42)[12] Jesus then allowed himself to be taken into custody, and stopped Peter from trying to prevent the arrest.[13]

Why was Jesus' death necessary? Even though Jesus voluntarily went to his death, despite the pain and suffering he knew would be involved, was his death truly necessary?

Jesus thought so: "Was it not necessary for the Christ to suffer these things and to enter into His glory?" (Luke 24:26)[14]

But why?

The New Testament speaks of Christ's death redeeming us and reconciling us to God.[15] His suffering saved us from our sins by granting us forgiveness and justification.[16] It also established a new covenant.[17] How did one man's death accomplish all of this? To find the answer to that question, we must plumb the depths of some often neglected portions of the Old and New Testaments.

We begin in the Garden of Eden,[18] where God commanded Adam and Eve not to eat from the tree of the knowledge of good and evil, "for in the day that you eat from it you will surely die." (Genesis 2:17) Their subsequent disobedience resulted in their spiritual estrangement from God—that is, their spiritual death. This estrangement was symbolized by their ejection from the Garden, and thus from God's presence.[19] The knowledge of good and evil brought the realization that they—and we—often fall on the "evil" side of that equation.

Ch. 12 – Did Jesus Really Have To Die?

We are all wrongdoers to a greater or lesser extent. As Paul said in Romans 3:23: "all have sinned and fall short of the glory of God." We have hurt each other, and ourselves, through our words and actions. And we have hurt God. For he not only knows what we have done, his omniscience means that he has felt the pain of those whom we have wounded.[20]

We sometimes try to excuse our wrongs by pointing out that "nobody's perfect." But the fact that others are similarly guilty does not make us any less so. Our innate sense of justice recognizes that wrongdoing must be punished—and not merely to deter others or rehabilitate the offender. Justice itself demands that a person pay for his crimes. Is it surprising that God's perfect justice requires the same?

So like Adam and Eve, our wrongdoing has resulted in our separation from the source of life. We are powerless to change this circumstance, for we can never erase our crimes or grant ourselves a pardon.

But God did not wish to leave us in this hopeless state of exile. Since he cannot change his nature or his standards, he had to find another way. He must forgive us and purify us. And that brings us to the concept of *atonement*.

Webster's New World Dictionary defines "atone" as "to make amends or reparation" for wrongdoing.[21] Just as a criminal must pay for breaking society's laws, we must all pay for disobeying God's laws.

In the Old Testament, atonement is achieved through the shedding of blood, as explained in Leviticus 17:11:

> For the life of the flesh is in the blood, and I have given it to you on the altar to make

atonement for your souls; for it is the blood by
reason of the life that makes atonement.

With only limited exceptions, atonement in the Old
Testament requires the shedding of blood.[22] Thus, we read in
Hebrews 9:22: "And according to the Law, *one may* almost
say, all things are cleansed with blood, and without shedding of blood there is no forgiveness." This sacrificial
atonement also served to purify and make things holy, as in
Exodus 29:35-37 (the altar), Leviticus 8:30-34 (Aaron and his
sons), and Leviticus 16:14-19 (the holy place inside the ta-
bernacle).

In his mercy, God decreed that the atoning blood
would be animal blood rather than human blood.[23] But the
author of Hebrews explains that this was only an imperfect
substitute, for the blood of animals "cannot make the wor-
shiper perfect in conscience" (Hebrews 9:9-10) or take away
sins.[24] Christ's blood can, and does.[25] Unlike the animal sacrifices offered annually on the Day of Atonement,[26] Jesus only
had to offer himself once—his death was sufficient.[27]

You may well ask, "How could one man's death save
all of mankind?" This may be a mystery beyond our comprehension. The New Testament simply states it as fact,
without explaining how it is possible. But we can speculate a
bit.

First, we must not minimize the magnitude of Jesus'
suffering. The New Testament says that we deserve God's
wrath for our wrongdoing, but Jesus saves us from that
wrath.[28] This implies that in addition to undergoing an ago-
nizing earthly death, he also endured God's wrath for our
wrongdoing—which was surely much worse. Perhaps that is
why he quoted Psalm 22:1 while hanging on the cross: "My

God, my God, why have You forsaken Me?" (Matthew 27:46)

Nor should we minimize the extent of his suffering. Jesus was no ordinary man. He claimed to be God, or at least God-like.[29] So we have no reason to believe that his memories fade like ours do. That humiliation, flogging, and crucifixion may be as real to him today as they were 2,000 years ago.

God was not immune to this torment, either (whether or not you accept the doctrine of the Trinity).[30] Just as he feels our pain, he must have felt Jesus' agony as well—and perhaps he still does.

Finally, there is the question of justice. How is God's justice satisfied by the killing of one who did no wrong, rather than the death of the wrongdoers? This might be another mystery beyond our comprehension. Yet two analogies may help us. One sees us as debtors, while the other treats us as criminals.

C.S. Lewis used the analogy of a debtor imprisoned by his creditors. As in Jesus' parable about the gracious king and the unforgiving slave,[31] we all owe a debt to God that we cannot pay. We need someone to pay our debt for us. Jesus' infinite worth enables him to do that.

However, I do not find that analogy wholly satisfying because I believe our situation is more like criminals who have violated the law—God's law. And as criminals, we need a pardon. Our own laws instruct us that such a pardon can only come from God.

Crimes are ultimately wrongs against society. Thus, criminal cases are phrased as "The State vs." or "The People vs." The victim of our crime cannot grant us a pardon. It must come from someone authorized to act on behalf of the society whose laws we have broken, such as the president or a governor.

Similarly, violations of God's laws require a pardon which must come from God. He has promised to grant that pardon to those who place their faith in Jesus Christ.

Yet the earlier question remains. How is justice served by Jesus receiving the punishment we deserve?

If we think of Jesus as merely an innocent bystander, or as the victim of our crimes, or even as our judge, then justice would not be satisfied. But he is much more. He is the king who wrote the law. And he decreed as part of that law that violations could be atoned for—and could *only* be atoned for—through the shedding of innocent blood. Jesus could accept our punishment in our place because his own law says that he can.

So Jesus' death was not a mistake. It was necessary to enable God to pardon us and to now embrace us as his children.

Ch. 12 – Did Jesus Really Have To Die?

Endnotes for Chapter Twelve, "Did Jesus Really Have To Die?"

1. Sun Myung Moon (1920 – 2012), a Korean, founded the Unification Church.

2. This is the implication of Matthew 26:36-46, Mark 14:32-42, and Luke 22:39-46. These verses talk about Jesus praying repeatedly in the Garden of Gethsemane while His disciples slept.

3. See Matthew 26:67, 27:2, 27:26-50; Mark 14:65, 15:1, 15:15-37; Luke 22:63, 23:11, 23:33-46; John 18:12, 18:22-24, 19:1-3, 19:16-18, 19:23-30.

4. John 19:31-32. The Romans did not break Jesus' legs because He was already dead. John 19:33

5. See also Mark 8:29 and Luke 9:20.

6. See also Mark 8:31, 9:31; Luke 9:22; and John 2:19-22.

7. Mark 10:33-34; see also Matthew 20:18-19, and Luke 18:32-33

8. Matthew 20:19 and Luke 24:6-7

9. When Jesus was tried by the Jewish Sanhedrin, the accusation was blasphemy, since He had claimed to be the Son of God. (Matthew 26:63-66; Mark 14:61-64; Luke 22:70-71; John 19:7) But a charge of blasphemy would not have impressed the Roman procurator, Pilate, and only the Romans had authority to order Jesus' death. (John 18:31) So the accusation the Jewish leaders brought to Pilate was that Jesus had claimed to be a king. (Matthew 27:11, 27:37; Mark 15:2, 15:9, 15:12, 15:26; Luke 23:2-3, 23:14, 23:36-38; John 18:33, 18:37, 19:14-15) Such a claim would be viewed as treason by the Romans in occupied Judea.

10. This occurred during what became known as the Last Supper—that is, Jesus' last meal before His death.

11. Matthew 26:26-29; Mark 14:22-25; Luke 22:14-20; and 1 Corinthians 11:23-26; see also, John 6:41-59, in which Jesus uses the same metaphor regarding His body and blood, but in a different context.

12. See also Matthew 26:39, Mark 14:36, and John 18:11.

13. Matthew 26:51-54; Luke 22:49-51; John 18:10-11

14. See also Luke 24:44-46.

15. Romans 5:10-11; Ephesians 2:16; Colossians 1:20-22; 1 Peter 1:18-19, 3:18; Revelation 5:9-10

16. Matthew 1:21, 26:28; Luke 24:47; Romans 3:24-26, 5:9; 1 Corinthians 15:3, 15:17; Galatians 1:3-4; Ephesians 1:7; Colossians 1;13-14, 2:13-14; Hebrews 1:3, 2:17, 7:27, 9:12-14, 9:26-28, 10:10-12, 13:12; 1 Peter 2:24; 1 John 1:7, 2:2, 4:10; Revelation 1:5

17. Matthew 26:28; Mark 22:24; Luke 22:20; 1 Corinthians 11:25; Hebrews 9:15, 10:29, 13:20

18. Whether you regard the story of Adam and Eve as history, allegory, or myth is unimportant for our present purposes. The basic truth the story teaches remains the same.

19. Genesis 3:22-24

20. For example, see Psalm 139 and Hebrews 4:12, which talk about God's omniscience.

21. Guralnik, *Webster's New World Dictionary of the American Language*, p. 88.

22. The exceptions to this general rule are as follows: Exodus 30:11-16 (atonement money); Leviticus 5:11-13 (flour given as a sin offering by those too poor to afford an animal or bird); Numbers 16:41-49 (Aaron stops a plague through fire from the altar and incense); Numbers 31:48-51 (atonement *apparently* made through the offering of booty to the Lord, although God did not explicitly sanction this); 2 Samuel 21:1-9 (seven descendants of King Saul hanged to make atonement for Saul's misdeeds; although this is an example of atonement without blood, it is not without death); Daniel 9:24 (exile of the Jews to Babylon; another example of atonement without blood, but not without punishment).

23. Exodus 29:10-14, 35-37, 30:6-10; Leviticus 1:1-5, 4:13-35, 5:1-10, 5:14-19, 6:1-7, 6:24-30, 7:1-7, 8:14-15, 8:30-34, 9:7, 10:16-20, 12:6-8, 14:10-31, 14:49-53, 15:13-15, 15:28-30, 16:5-11, 16:14-19, 16:27, 19:20-22, 23:26-28; Numbers 5:5-8, 6:9-11, 8:12, 15:22-28, 28:16-22, 28:26-30, 29:5, 29:11; 1 Chronicles 6:49; 2Chronicles 29:20-24; Nehemiah 10:32-33; Ezekiel 43:18-20, 43:25-26, 45:13-20. See also Leviticus 4:1-7, in which atonement through the shedding of animal blood is implied.

24. Hebrews 10:1-4; see also Hebrews 7:18-19

25. Hebrews 1:3, 2:17, 9:13-14, 9:25-28, 10:10; see also Romans 3:25, 1 John 2:2, and 1 John 4:10.

26. Exodus 30:10; Leviticus 16:2-34, 23:26-28

27. Hebrews 9:25-28, 10:10-14; see also 1 Peter 3:18.

28. See, for example: John 3:36; Romans 1:18, 2:5, 2:8, 4:15, 5:9; Ephesians 2:3, 5:6; Colossians 3:6; 1 Thessalonians 1:10, 5:9; Revelation 6:15-17, 14:19.

29. Jesus' claims of divinity are discussed in Chapter One ("Christianity Is Different") of my book, *Beyond Blind Faith: Reasons for the Hope We Have (1 Peter 3:15)*. Briefly, those claims were: (1) He thought He was perfect; (2) He claimed to be eternal; (3) He said He was the Christ (Messiah), the Son of God, and He considered himself equal with God; (4) He taught that following or rejecting him was the same as following or rejecting God; (5) He insisted that He had come from Heaven, and He spoke about Heaven as if He'd been there; (6) He predicted His own death—and, more importantly, His resurrection; (7) He believed His death was necessary to save the world; (8) He claimed to have authority to forgive sins; and (9) He didn't bother to cite any type of authority to validate what He said or did.

30. The Trinity is a difficult theological doctrine that asserts that the Father, Son, and Holy Spirit are three persons, but only one God. St. Patrick used the analogy of a clover—three leaves, but only one plant. Not being a theologian or a clergyman myself, I will not attempt to explain the doctrine of the Trinity further. Please consult your priest, pastor, or minister.

31. Matthew 18:23-35; Jesus uses a similar analogy in Luke 7:40-48.

Chapter 13
PASCAL'S WAGER REVISITED

Blaise Pascal[1] was a French mathematician, scientist, and philosopher—and a Christian. Some of his notes, posthumously published as *Pensées*, contained the argument for belief in God which has been nicknamed, "Pascal's wager." The argument contends that we should believe God exists because we lose nothing if we are wrong, but gain everything—i.e., eternal life, Heaven, eternal joy and happiness—if we are right. On the other hand, denying that God exists gains us nothing if we are right, but would result in eternal misery if we are wrong.

During my high school days, a close friend of mine tried to convince me to become a Christian by invoking Pascal's wager. It didn't work. And it shouldn't.

The argument is flawed in at least two respects. First, recall from Chapter Ten ("Is Free Will an Illusion?") that God wants far more than our mere intellectual acknowledgement of his existence. The greatest commandment is: "YOU SHALL LOVE THE LORD YOUR GOD WITH ALL YOUR HEART, AND WITH ALL YOUR SOUL, AND WITH ALL YOUR MIND." (Matthew 22:37, quoting Deuteronomy 6:5) God wants us to love him as he loves us, so that he can have a loving relationship with us—like a parent and child.

We also discussed in Chapter Ten that God wants our trust. The New Testament word translated as the English "believe" and "faith" is the Greek word, *pistis*, or its verb form *pisteuô*, which connotes trust and commitment. God wants us to trust him and commit our lives to him—and he has promised to give eternal life to those who do so.[2]

So Pascal's wager is flawed by asking us to do too little—to merely give an intellectual nod to God's existence rather than to love and trust him. But let us give Monsieur Pascal the benefit of the doubt. Perhaps he assumed that "belief" in God would naturally be accompanied by trust in God, and eventually love of God. His wager is still flawed because it minimizes what we truly lose if God does not exist.

The apostle Paul recognized this. In Chapter 15 of his first letter to the Corinthians, he sought to refute those who denied that a physical resurrection such as Jesus' could occur. Then he added in verse 19: "If we have hoped in Christ in this life only, we are of all men most to be pitied." Paul knew better than most that committing your life to God and to Christ involves many sacrifices.

For one thing, the Christian will face the world's scorn: "Do not be surprised, brethren, if the world hates you." (1 John 3:13)[3] In the first three centuries of Christianity, such hatred often resulted in persecution—from the Jews at first, and later from the Romans. Such persecution could involve loss of property, loss of position, imprisonment, torture, exile, and even death. Paul suffered as much as anyone, as he explained in his second letter to the Corinthians:

> Are they servants of Christ?—I speak as if insane—I more so; in far more labors, in far more imprisonments, beaten times without number, often in danger of death. Five times I received from the Jews thirty-nine *lashes*. Three times I was beaten with rods, once I was stoned, three times I was shipwrecked, a night and a day I

have spent in the deep. *I have been* on frequent journeys, in dangers from rivers, dangers from robbers, dangers from *my* countrymen, dangers from the Gentiles, dangers in the city, dangers in the wilderness, dangers on the sea, dangers among false brethren; *I have been* in labor and hardship, through many sleepless nights, in hunger and thirst, often without food, in cold and exposure.

—2 Corinthians 11:23-27

Paul was eventually executed for his faith in about 64 A.D., as was the apostle Peter. The book of Acts records a similar fate suffered by Stephen and James the son of Zebedee (also known as James the Greater).[4] According to reliable traditions, many of Jesus' apostles and early disciples were killed because of their faith.[5]

If God does not exist, these people threw away their lives for nothing.[6]

That was then and this is now, yet Christians continue to be persecuted in countries around the world—particularly in China and some Muslim countries.[7]

In places which enjoy freedom of religion, such overt hatred and persecution is rare. Less rare is the belittling of the Christian narrative and the criticism of Christian values by secular culture, which sometimes leaves Christians feeling alienated from society.

Over and above whatever persecution Christians may suffer or perceive, true believers in Christ forsake many things the world considers desirable—like the selfish pursuit of wealth. Human nature tells us to seek security through money, but the Christian finds his security in God. Jesus considered wealth to be an impediment to devotion to God, for "You cannot serve God and wealth" (Matthew 6:24).[8] Jesus actually advised some to impoverish themselves for the sake of God's kingdom.[9] Paul summarized the New Testament attitude toward money in 1 Timothy 6:10: "For the love of money is a root of all sorts of evil, and some by longing for it have wandered away from the faith and pierced themselves with many griefs."[10]

Similarly, human nature tells us we should focus primarily on our own welfare—watch out for number one. Jesus instead called upon his followers to become servants, selflessly giving to help others, especially those who are less fortunate:

> But Jesus called them to Himself and said, "You know that the rulers of the Gentiles lord it over them, and their great men exercise authority over them. It is not this way among you, but whoever wishes to become great among you shall be your servant, and whoever wishes to be first among you shall be your slave, just as the Son of Man did not come to be served, but to serve, and to give His life a ransom for many."
>
> —Matthew 20:25-28[11]

> Then they themselves also will answer, "Lord, when did we see You hungry, or thirsty, or a stranger, or naked, or sick, or in prison, and did not take care of You?" Then He [the Son of Man] will answer them, "Truly I say to you, to

> the extent that you did not do it to one of the
> least of these, you did not do it to Me."
> —Matthew 25:44-45[12]

Matthew 16:24 aptly sums up this self-sacrificial attitude: "If anyone wishes to come after Me, he must deny himself, and take up his cross and follow Me."[13]

The New Testament also implores Christians to behave in ways that most non-Christians would consider foolish. For example, we have seen in previous chapters[14] that Jesus disapproves of divorce,[15] revenge,[16] grudges,[17] judging others,[18] anger and insults,[19] and lust outside of marriage.[20]

In Galatians 5:19-23, Paul provides a laundry list of vices Christians are to avoid and virtues they are to emulate:

> Now the deeds of the flesh are evident, which
> are: immorality, impurity, sensuality, idolatry,
> sorcery, enmities, strife, jealousy, outbursts of
> anger, disputes, dissensions, factions, envying,
> drunkenness, carousing, and things like these,
> of which I forewarn you, just as I have fore-
> warned you, that those who practice such
> things will not inherit the kingdom of God. But
> the fruit of the Spirit is love, joy, peace, pa-
> tience, kindness, goodness, faithfulness, gen-
> tleness, self-control; against such things there is
> no law.

Jesus' and Paul's standards are difficult to meet. How many non-believers would even want to try?

So Pascal's wager turns out to be a false choice. Monsieur Pascal would have you believe that choosing to follow Christ is as easy and painless as deciding to change your shirt. Neither the Christian message nor the Christian life is so simple—although I will add that I would not want to live my life any other way.

Monsieur Pascal chose a gambling metaphor to express his view of the choice we all face. I prefer a different metaphor. Imagine that you are in a burning building, and a fireman arrives to lead you to safety. Do you follow him, despite the danger you might face, and even though you do not know the path he will take?

We are all in a burning building called life, and Christ is the fireman who offers us a way of escape. We can choose to remain in the building and eventually die, or we can follow Christ and be saved—and receive eternal life. The latter requires that we trust him, just as we must trust the fireman who wants to lead us to safety. But the alternative is certain death. I am following the fireman.

Endnotes for Chapter Thirteen, "Pascal's Wager Revisited"

1. 1623-1662

2. As I have stated before, I leave to God what happens to non-believers. I do not believe I am in a position to make that call—nor is anyone else on earth.

3. See also Matthew 5:11-12, 10:22, 24:9; Mark 13:13; Luke 6:22, 21:17; John 15:18-19; 1 Peter 4:12-14.

4. Acts 7:54-60 and 12:1-2.

5. Christians suffered intermittent persecution at the hands of the Romans for almost three-hundred years. Such persecutions ended in the western Roman Empire when Constantine, Emperor of the western Roman Empire, issued the Edict of Milan in 313 A.D. The persecutions continued in the eastern Roman Empire until about 323 A.D. when Constantine united the Empire under his rule.

6. Indeed, as I discuss in Chapter Two of my book, *Beyond Blind Faith*, entitled "Is Jesus' Resurrection Fact or Fairy Tale?," if God does not exist these people threw their lives away for a lie. They preached all over the Roman Empire and beyond that Jesus had been raised from the dead, which was obviously a lie if there is no God.

7. Several verses explicitly warn—and others imply—that Christians should expect persecution. See, for example, Matthew 5:10-12, 5:44, 10:23, 13:21, 23:34; Mark 4:17, 10:30; Luke 21:12; John 15:20; Romans 8:35, 12:14; 1 Corinthians 4:12; 2 Corinthians 4:8-9, 12:10; Galatians 6:12; 2 Timothy 3:12.

8. See also Matthew 6:19-21; Mark 10:23-25; Luke 16:13, 18:24-25.

9. See, for example, Matthew 19:16-21; Mark 10:17-22; Luke 12:33-34, 18:18-22

10. See also 1 Timothy 3:2-3; Hebrews 13:5.

11. See also Matthew 23:11; Mark 9:35, 10:42-45; Luke 22:25-27; Galatians 5:13-14.

12. The full parable is found at Matthew 25:31-46. See also James 2:15-16.

13. See also Matthew 10:38; Mark 8:34; Luke 9:23, 14:27.

14. For example, Chapters Five ("Rebellion and Repentance"), Eight ("You Don't Deserve This"), and Ten ("Is Free Will an Illusion?")

15. Matthew 5:31-32; see also Matthew 19:9; Mark 10:11-12; Luke 16:18; 1 Corinthians 7:11.

16. Matthew 5:39-41; see also Luke 6:29; 1 Corinthians 6:7

17. See also Luke 6:27-28, 23:34; Acts 7:60; Romans 12:20.

18. Matthew 7:1-5; see also Luke 6:37-38, 6:41-42; Romans 14:1-4, 14:10, 14:13

19. Matthew 5:22

20. Matthew 5:28

Chapter 14
God's Oasis in Space

For since the creation of the world His invisible attributes, His eternal power and divine nature, have been clearly seen, being understood through what has been made, so that they are without excuse.

—Romans 1:20

The heavens are telling of the glory of God;
And their expanse is declaring the work of His
hands.

—Psalm 19:1

If you want evidence of God's awesome power, just listen to what astronomers tell us the universe contains. Near the far side of the known universe, quasars[1] generate the energetic equivalent of a galactic explosion. Throughout the universe—even in our own Milky Way Galaxy—we find stellar collisions, exploding stars called supernovas,[2] black holes,[3] and deadly levels of radiation. Any of these would obliterate life[4] on Earth if they occurred within a few light-years[5] of us.

On the other hand, if you want proof of God's grace, look at Earth. Life exists on this planet only because God created an oasis amid the desert of space. In this chapter we will explore the lengths to which he went to provide a hospitable planet for us.

Our Place in the Galaxy. Astronomers believe the center of our Milky Way Galaxy, like most galactic centers, harbors a super-massive black hole that can gobble up matter equivalent to the mass[6] of our Sun each 5,000 years. The region within 40 parsecs,[7] or about 130 light-years, of that galactic center is called the galactic nucleus. That area is a shooting gallery of deadly forces, such as violent fast-moving gases, stellar collisions, and lethal levels of radiation.[8]

To keep us alive, God placed Earth roughly 24,000 light-years from the galactic center, two-thirds of the way to the galaxy's edge. That's a good place to be, because things are much calmer out here. Where we are, other stars are at a safe distance—the nearest star system to us, the Alpha Centauri system, is more than four light-years away—so we face no realistic danger of another star colliding with our Sun or passing close enough to wreak havoc on our planet.

The Sun. Speaking of the Sun, God put us in orbit around an ideal star. Like all stars, the Sun is an enormous ball of hydrogen gas. Because of gravity, that hydrogen is compressed to the point that hydrogen atoms near the center fuse into helium atoms, releasing energy. This is called nuclear fusion—the same nuclear fusion that creates the blast in a hydrogen bomb. The Sun powers our world from ninety-three million miles away because it converts hundreds of millions of tons of hydrogen into helium every second.

The Sun is a medium-sized star, which means that it will never explode like a supernova. That only happens with stars that are several times as massive as the Sun. Larger stars also generate a lot more ultraviolet (UV) radiation. A high level of UV radiation is harmful, and potentially fatal, for living organisms because it breaks down most biological molecules. UV radiation makes up only about ten percent of the energy the Sun emits, whereas with larger, hotter stars the level approaches one-hundred percent. As we will see, God has provided us with a lot of protection from the Sun's UV radiation, but higher levels would present a much greater danger.

So we can be thankful that the Sun is not larger than it is. On the other hand, we would not want it to be much smaller, either, for such stars are often unstable, sending out bursts of radiation that could annihilate life on Earth. In addition, if the Sun were smaller, Earth would probably need to orbit closer in order to receive sufficient solar energy to keep the planet livable. But a closer orbit risks what astronomers call "tidal locking," which means that the gravitational pull of the larger body brings the planet's spin to a near stop and synchronizes its rotation with its orbit. Earth has done that to the Moon. Because of Earth's gravity, the same side of the Moon always faces Earth, and the other side is always dark. In the absence of an abundance of greenhouse gases, the atmosphere freezes when a planet has a permanently dark side.[9]

Our Sun is quite stable, as stars go, emitting a fairly constant level of heat and light. Many stars lack this stability. They are called "variable stars," since their brightness—and hence the amount of heat and light they emit—varies, often on a regular schedule. The heat and light of some variable stars fluctuate because of changes in their surface temperature, while others actually expand and contract. Still others expel part of their mass into space. These variations can be subtle or quite dramatic.[10] Whatever the cause, the ever-changing heat and light of these variable stars would likely be devastating for most living organisms, especially our fragile species, homo sapiens.

The Sun is a "Goldilocks" star. Not too hot or too cold, it emits just the right amount of heat and light to support life. "Perhaps 15 percent of the stars in the Galaxy have the proper mass to be just luminous enough—but not too luminous—to support habitable planets."[11]

We can also thank God that our Sun is a solitary star—a decided exception in the universe where most stars are either in a binary system (two stars orbiting each other) or a multi-star system (more than two stars in orbit around each other).[12] For example, the Alpha Centauri star system consists of three stars—two orbiting each other, and a third orbiting those two. In our Milky Way Galaxy, only about ten to fifteen percent of the stars are solitary.

Many astronomers believe that a solitary star system is safer for life, because the competing gravitational forces of two or more stars can cause problems for a planet in such a system—for example, showering it with rogue asteroids and comets, subjecting it to wild temperature swings, creating an erratic or highly elliptical orbit, pulling it into one of the stars, or ejecting it from the solar system into cold, dark space.[13] Of these possibilities, rogue asteroids and comets might seem the least worrisome, yet they are a serious threat.

A chance encounter with a large asteroid or a comet can be devastating. For example, an asteroid (or perhaps a comet) about six miles in diameter, hurtling toward Earth at a speed in excess of 60,000 miles an hour, probably caused the extinction of the dinosaurs sixty-five million years ago— along with at least half of the species then living on Earth.[14]

That asteroid (or comet) packed the punch of 100 million hydrogen bombs. It generated an impact crater on and near the Yucatan Peninsula more than 100 miles across, produced a fireball that incinerated large portions of the United States and Mexico, initiated a tsunami more than a half-mile high, started fires over most of the planet, and cast so much dust and smoke into the atmosphere that darkness and cold enveloped Earth for months.

The climate later heated to uncomfortable temperature levels due to the greenhouse effect of enormous amounts of carbon dioxide (CO_2) and water vapor expelled into the atmosphere during and after the impact. The CO_2 came not only from fires and decomposition of dead plants and animals, but also from the asteroid's (or comet's) evisceration of much of the Yucatan's limestone, which releases CO_2 when it breaks down.

In addition, the super-heated air compressed by the asteroid's approach probably catalyzed the formation of nitrous oxide—atmospheric nitrogen combined with oxygen—which turned ordinary precipitation into acid rain. This acid rain was made more toxic because it also included an abundance of sulfur from the area that was struck.

Earth may not have returned to its former idyllic state for hundreds of years.[15]

Our Place in the Solar System. While another such impact is always possible,[16] God has given us a measure of protection through our big brother, Jupiter. It is the largest planet in the solar system, with a mass of more than 300 Earths.[17] As such, its powerful gravitational field has attracted, and continues to attract, many asteroids and comets that might otherwise threaten us.[18] Without Jupiter, the frequency of impacts by large asteroids and comets would be much greater. Saturn has similar beneficial effects, though to a lesser degree since it has only about one-third the mass of Jupiter.[19]

Nor do we need to worry about colliding with another planet, for God has arranged the orbits of the planets in our solar system so that they are nearly circular rather than sharply elliptical. This avoids planetary collisions—which would almost certainly be fatal for life on Earth—because the planetary orbits do not cross.

A nearly circular orbit is also beneficial because it keeps Earth from experiencing temperature extremes, as would be the case if our distance from the Sun varied greatly.

Real estate is all about location, and God has placed Earth in an ideal location within the solar system. We are far enough from the Sun that we are not superheated like Mercury and Venus, but not so far away that we are a cold, dead planet like Mars. James Kasting, an astrobiologist, estimates that Earth's temperature would not have been suitable for most animal life, including humans, if the distance from Earth to the Sun—which is ninety-three million miles—had been about five million miles less or about fourteen million miles more.[20] In large part because of our location—but also because of our greenhouse gases, which we will talk about later—Earth has liquid water, without which life as we know it would not exist.[21]

Earth's Magnetosphere. A comet consists primarily of ice—frozen water—along with small amounts of frozen methane, frozen ammonia, and various minerals. Most comets have extreme elliptical orbits around the Sun, spending most of their lives beyond Neptune—some *way* beyond Neptune.[22] As a comet approaches the Sun, its icy surface warms and partially melts, throwing off a tail which trails behind the nucleus. But when the comet completes its trip around the Sun and begins the journey back to the outer limits of our Solar System, something unexpected happens: its tail no longer trails behind, but actually goes in front—that is, away from the Sun.

Why? The solar wind.

The solar wind consists of a constant stream of particles—mostly protons and electrons—traveling away from the Sun at a speed in excess of 300 miles per second (that's faster than one million miles per hour). Scientists believe the solar wind may have stripped Mars of most of its atmosphere. The same thing has not happened to Earth because God gave us a strong magnetic field—the magnetosphere.[23]

The magnetosphere is like a giant magnet generated by our planet's rotation and its core of liquid iron. This magnetic field extends well beyond our atmosphere and deflects most of the solar wind. The few particles that do manage to get through are deflected toward the north and south poles, where they are drained of their energy by impacts with air molecules in the atmosphere, creating the Aurora Borealis, or Northern Lights, and the Aurora Australis, the Southern Lights.

Earth's Stratosphere.[24] Although the Sun nourishes us with a constant flow of heat and light, our favorite star is not entirely benign. The Sun's ultraviolet (UV) radiation gives us sunburn when we forget to wear sunscreen at the beach, and long-term exposure causes skin cancer. Yet we receive only a small fraction of the UV radiation the Sun sends our way.

The full dose would kill. So God gave Earth an ozone[25] layer to shield us.

Ozone, residing in the stratosphere many miles above Earth's surface, absorbs 97 to 99 percent of that deadly UV radiation.[26] When scientists discovered that man-made chlorofluorocarbons (CFCs) were slowly destroying the ozone layer,[27] world leaders agreed to quit using CFCs in developed countries by 1996. The ozone layer now seems to be repairing itself and may return to 1980 levels by the middle of this century.

Earth's Atmosphere. Aside from the magnetosphere, Earth has an atmosphere because the planet is sufficiently massive to hold onto one. Mars, with only one-tenth the mass of Earth, has lost most of its atmosphere, which is one percent as dense as our own.

God gave us an atmosphere composed of 78% nitrogen, 21% oxygen, and 1% everything else. Having plenty of oxygen is good, since without it all animal life would perish. God also gave us abundant plant life to continuously replenish the atmospheric oxygen, which would otherwise become depleted.[28] Plants do this through the amazing—we could even say miraculous—process of photosynthesis, which uses CO_2, water, and the Sun's energy to produce carbohydrates such as glucose, releasing oxygen as a by-product. By the way, some of God's humblest creatures—algae and single-celled organisms called cyanobacteria—are responsible for more than half of this photosynthesis, and thus a great deal of the oxygen we breathe. Cyanobacteria are a form of plankton.[29]

While oxygen is a good thing, God was careful not to give us too much of it. Breathing high levels of oxygen for extended periods of time can damage eyes, lungs, and the central nervous system, as well as various other organs. It can even result in death. And if oxygen were too plentiful, fires would start and spread with little provocation.

Nitrogen, the primary component of our atmosphere, is one of the main ingredients in nitrates, which plants convert into proteins. Without nitrates, we would have no plants—and pretty soon no animals or human beings either. While we are at it, God thought to create bacteria and algae that can extract nitrogen from the air and convert it into a form that plants can use,[30] because multi-cellular plants cannot extract nitrogen from the air on their own.

In that one percent of our atmosphere that doesn't consist of oxygen or nitrogen, God added small amounts of carbon dioxide, water vapor, and other greenhouse gases (such as methane) to trap enough of the Sun's energy to give us a pleasant average global temperature of just under 60° F. Without them, Earth would have an average temperature of about 0° F and would be an ice planet. These gases also keep us from experiencing the extreme temperature swings of Mercury, Mars, and the Moon.[31]

The density of our atmosphere is ideal, too. It protects us from smaller meteors because they burn up as they descend through our atmosphere. Mars' thin atmosphere provides almost no protection for the planet surface, which is marred by obvious impact craters. On the other hand, our atmosphere is much less dense than that of Venus, whose atmospheric pressure is approximately ninety times as great as Earth's.[32] Venus' atmospheric pressure would literally crush the life out of us.

Plate tectonics. God gave us a natural thermostat to regulate the global temperature and keep it within livable limits: the carbon cycle.[33] This thermostat primarily operates by adjusting the amount of carbon dioxide (CO_2) in the atmosphere. Since carbon dioxide is one of the greenhouse gases, adding CO_2 warms the planet and removing CO_2 has the opposite effect. The process through which this happens is called "weathering."

Weathering is a chemical reaction that generates limestone from minerals known as silicates. Atmospheric CO_2 naturally dissolves in bodies of water—rivers, lakes, and oceans—where it reacts with water to form carbonic acid. Weathering happens when this carbonic acid reacts with silicate minerals in submerged rocks to form limestone. The rate of weathering increases as the temperature warms, which results in more CO_2 being captured and locked away in limestone—leaving less to warm the planet. When the temperature cools, weathering slows, more CO_2 remains in the atmosphere, and we warm again. The captured CO_2 gets recycled through the process of plate tectonics[34] and subduction.

To understand plate tectonics we must start near the center of the earth, where heat generated by the decay of radioactive materials melts dense rock deep inside the planet. Since heat rises, this liquid rock climbs toward the surface, releases some of its heat, and then sinks back toward the center of the earth where it is reheated.

Sitting on top of this circulating molten rock, like oil on top of water, are low-density land masses called "plates." These plates vary in thickness from about thirty to sixty miles. The circulation of the molten rock underneath causes these plates to move, but at the leisurely pace of only one or two inches per year.

When two of these plates collide, the impact pushes land upward, generating mountains and continents, while other land is forced downward toward the earth's interior. The latter is called subduction, and it is vital to recycling important molecules, including CO_2. Limestone that is subducted breaks down into its component parts. These components, including carbon dioxide, are then returned to the surface of the earth—primarily through volcanic eruptions, most of which occur along the edges of the plates where they collide, pull apart, or grind against each other. Without plate tectonics and subduction, most limestone would simply get buried and never recycled.[35]

Plants help this thermostat work more efficiently because they remove carbon dioxide from the atmosphere through photosynthesis. A warmer planet and more abundant CO_2 makes plants grow faster—at least, up to a point—which removes CO_2 at a faster rate.

By creating new land, plate tectonics also helps recycle nutrients that plants need to survive and thrive. Without plate tectonics, erosion would eventually carry most nutrients to the bottom of the ocean.

The Solid Rock Upon Which I Stand. Jupiter is the most massive planet in our solar system, but not the densest. That honor goes to none other than our own planet Earth. Jupiter, Saturn, Uranus, and Neptune are called "gas-giants" because they are mostly composed of gases like hydrogen, helium, and methane. Such an environment would be quite hostile to living organisms. So God made Earth a rocky planet instead of a gas-giant.

Earth's Rotation. Our planet rotates once every twenty-four hours, and we take this for granted. But if Earth rotated as slowly as Venus, which completes one rotation every 243 days, one side of the planet would bake under constant sunshine for months while the other side froze solid.

On the other hand, what if Earth rotated faster than it does—say, one revolution every four to six hours? That is what many scientists believe was the norm early in Earth's history, before the Moon slowed down the rotation. If Earth still spun that fast today, few people, if any, would be able to live near the equator. The faster spin would intensify the centrifugal force near the equator, drawing more ocean water there and submerging most or all of the land.

For the rest of us, we would obviously have shorter days and nights. But we would also have more dangerous hurricanes because of increased wind speeds, and more severe earthquakes because the tectonic plates would move faster. So let us be glad that God made the day twenty-four hours long.

While we are at it, God has blessed us with a large Moon. The Moon's diameter is about one-fourth that of Earth, and is as big as some of the moons of the gas-giants Jupiter and Saturn. Having a large Moon does two useful things for us besides slowing down our rotation. First, its gravity, along with that of the Sun, produces high and low tides, which many forms of life depend upon.

Second, it helps stabilize the wobble in Earth's rotation—in other words, it helps maintain Earth's twenty-three-degree tilt. That tilt is the reason for the seasons. During summer months the northern hemisphere is tilted toward the Sun, giving us more direct sunlight and warmer temperatures. In winter, we are tilted away from the Sun, which appears lower in the sky, giving us less direct sunlight and colder temperatures. (In the southern hemisphere, the effect is reversed—our summer is their winter, and vice versa.)

Without the Moon, astronomers believe the gravitational forces of the Sun and Jupiter could cause Earth's tilt to vary by as much as ninety degrees.[36] Imagine experiencing the North Pole's twenty-four-hour winter darkness in Chicago, or having the summer Sun directly overhead in Juneau, Alaska. Keeping Earth's tilt at twenty-three degrees minimizes fluctuations in our climate.[37]

Water. Water is amazing. Perhaps its most remarkable quality is that its liquid form is denser than its solid form. In other words, ice floats. If it did not, it would sink and fill the bottoms of lakes, rivers, and oceans, wiping out most of the life in its way and leaving much less water for the use of living organisms.

Another marvelous quality water possesses is its high specific heat,[38] which simply means that a lot of energy is required to raise the temperature of water. Its specific heat is twice that of oil and five times that of aluminum. Because of water's high specific heat, it doesn't heat or cool very fast, which keeps the surrounding air temperature relatively constant. This helps moderate the planet's temperature. It also makes water incredibly useful for living organisms by enabling them to maintain a fairly stable internal temperature.[39]

Water is an excellent solvent. This means that a lot of substances will easily dissolve in it,[40] including most of the chemicals essential for life. This is critical because many of these chemicals can enter a cell only as part of a solution.

Another useful property is water's neutral pH. Unlike most other liquids water is neither an acid nor a base.[41] Both acids and bases can be useful to living organisms under the right circumstances—for example, stomach acid helps us digest foods.[42] However, our body's cells, like those of most other living organisms, need a close-to-neutral pH to function properly.[43] Strong acids and bases can be harmful—or even fatal if they are strong enough. Water, with its neutral pH, carries no such risk, which must be one reason God made it the foundation of all life.

Water is necessary for many of the chemical reactions required by living organisms. The most prominent of these are photosynthesis and respiration. Recall that through photosynthesis plants use water and carbon dioxide to make carbohydrates and oxygen. In respiration, animals use oxygen to break down carbohydrates into water and CO_2, which releases energy animals can use. Photosynthesis is thus the foundation of the food chain.[44] If water did not exist on Earth, photosynthesis would be impossible.

Since life on Earth cannot survive long without water, God made sure we had an abundant supply of it. Water covers about three-quarters of the surface of the earth, ensuring that we do not become a lifeless desert planet like Mercury or Mars.

On the other hand, he did not give us too much water. If Earth had twice as much water as it does, the land would be completely covered.

Too much water could also disrupt the carbon cycle—Earth's thermostat—because carbonic acid and silicates combine to form limestone most efficiently in shallow water. If only deep water were available, carbon dioxide might

173

build up in the atmosphere and turn Earth into a hot, unlivable planet like Venus.

Conclusion. Many scientists, atheists, and amateur philosophers hope we will one day find evidence of life, possibly even intelligent life, somewhere in the universe. Perhaps we will, although the search has been unsuccessful so far.

Regardless of whether or not we ever find other forms of life in the universe, we should appreciate the lengths to which God went to create an environment in which life could exist and flourish here. If God were to withdraw his protection for even a short time, life would cease to exist. Job said it well:

> But now ask the beasts, and let them teach you;
> And the birds of the heavens, and let them tell you.
> Or speak to the earth, and let it teach you;
> And let the fish of the sea declare to you.
> Who among all these does not know
> That the hand of the LORD has done this,
> In whose hand is the life of every living thing,
> And the breath of all mankind?
>
> —Job 12:7-10

When you pray tonight, thank God for the gift of life and for everything he has done to make life on Earth possible.

Ch. 14 – God's Oasis in Space

1. "Quasar" is an acronym for "quasi-stellar radio source." Because not all quasars emit powerful radio waves, they are also known as QSOs, short for "quasi-stellar object." The closest quasar is about five-hundred million light-years from us.

2. A supernova is a huge explosion that occurs when a massive star—much more massive than our Sun—nears the end of its life, collapses in on itself, and then explodes. A supernova can be bright enough to out-shine billions of stars. The temperature in the core of a supernova just before it explodes can reach one-hundred billion degrees Kelvin. After the explosion, whatever is left becomes either a neutron star or, if the matter is sufficiently dense and massive, a black hole. Chinese records of a supernova in the constellation Taurus in 1054 A.D. state that a "star" was so bright that it was visible in broad daylight for a month. The last supernova in our galaxy was in 1604 A.D.

3. A black hole is so incredibly dense and massive that not even light can escape its gravity. Since light is trapped, a black hole cannot be seen, but its gravitational effects can be measured.

4. Throughout this chapter, when I speak of "life" I do not include those microbial forms of life—so called "extremophiles"—which are able to survive under extreme conditions that would be fatal to higher forms of life including humans. These microbes can withstand heat in excess of 212° F (the boiling point of water), cold below 32° F (the freezing point of water), and seemingly toxic environments.

5. The speed of light is 186,282 miles per second in the vacuum of space. This is more than 670 million miles per hour. Light is slowed slightly when traveling through our atmosphere—to about 186,220 miles per second.

6. Mass is similar to, but different from, weight. Mass measures the amount of matter in a body, whereas weight measures the force of gravity on a body. Thus, going to the Moon is a great way to lose weight, because the weaker gravitational field there means you would weigh about one-sixth of what you do on Earth. But your mass would remain unchanged.

7. A parsec is about 3.26 light-years.

8. Radiation, like other forms of energy, dissipates as it travels, weakening as the square of the distance traveled. Thus, the energy becomes only one-quarter as strong each time distance doubles. For example, radiation two light-years from the source would be sixteen times stronger than it would be eight light-years from the source.

9. The two closest planets to the Sun have very slow rotation periods compared to Earth. Mercury takes more than 58 Earth days to complete a single rotation. Venus is even slower, requiring 243 days per rotation.

10. "Cataclysmic variables" can become many times brighter than their normal brightness, caused by thermonuclear explosions.

11. DePree and Axelrod, *Idiot's Guide to Astronomy*, p. 266

12. If Jupiter had been about eighty times larger, it would have possessed sufficient mass to become a star, and we would have been part of a binary star system. As is, Jupiter's enormous gravitational forces generate enough heat inside Europa, one of its moons, to create an ocean of liquid water beneath its frozen surface, merely by flexing the moon's interior.

13. We can also be thankful that God placed Jupiter and Saturn where He did. If Jupiter were closer to the Sun—say, where Venus or Mars is—its massive gravity would probably have a disruptive impact similar to that of a second Sun. If Saturn were a lot closer to Jupiter, the gravitational interplay between those two planets could radically change their orbits, with unpredictable dangers for Earth.

14. An asteroid or a comet was also responsible for an explosion that destroyed more than 750 square miles of Siberian forest on June 30, 1908—what is known as the Tunguska Event, the largest event of its kind in recorded history.

15. Much of the foregoing discussion about this disastrous asteroid (or comet) collision with Earth is summarized from Alvarez, *T. rex and the Crater of Doom*, pp. 5-15. Mr. Alvarez's explanation of the event is riveting, and I highly recommend it.

16. An object that does not burn up in our atmosphere and impacts the surface of the Earth is called a meteorite. Perhaps as many as 300,000 meteorites strike the Earth every year, but the vast majority fall harmlessly into the oceans or into uninhabited areas, and very few are large enough to do any real harm.

17. Jupiter's mass is dwarfed by that of the Sun, which is 1,000 times more. The Sun contains 99.9% of all of the mass in the solar system.

18. For example, in 1994 Jupiter attracted fragments from Comet Shoemaker-Levy 9, which crashed into Jupiter's atmosphere in a series of powerful explosions over a six-day period.

19. Saturn has the mass of about 95 Earths.

20. Ward & Brownlee, *Rare Earth*, p. 19.

21. Astronomers call this area where water can exist in its liquid state the "habitable zone."

22. Some comets are so far from the Sun that they take millions of years to complete one orbit around the Sun.

23. Mars has a magnetosphere, but it is too weak to protect the planet's atmosphere from the solar wind.

24. Earth's atmosphere is commonly divided into five layers:

    1. Troposphere – From the Earth's surface to between five and nine miles above the Earth's surface. This is where all of the breathable oxygen is.

    2. Stratosphere – From the top of the troposphere to about thirty-one miles above the Earth's surface. The ozone layer resides here.

    3. Mesosphere – From the top of the stratosphere to about fifty-three miles above the Earth's surface. Meteors generally burn up at this level.

    4. Thermosphere – From the top of the mesosphere to about 372 miles above the Earth's surface. Satellites orbit at this level, and the Aurora Borealis and the Aurora Australis occur here.

    5. Exosphere – From the top of the thermosphere to about 6,200 miles above the Earth's surface.

25. Ozone consists of three oxygen molecules—O_3. The oxygen we breath contains only two oxygen molecules—O_2.

26. We would not want *all* UV radiation to be blocked, because exposure to small amounts helps our bodies produce vitamin D.

27. CFCs were an ingredient in many refrigerants and aerosols. In the stratosphere, ultraviolet radiation breaks down CFC molecules, freeing up its chlorine atoms. The chlorine then steals one of the oxygen atoms

from an ozone molecule, producing chlorine monoxide and plain oxygen. In this way, ozone is destroyed.

28. Without plants, Earth would have little or no *atmospheric* oxygen. If plants were not constantly replenishing oxygen in the atmosphere, oxidation of other elements, as well as chemical reactions with atmospheric nitrogen, would soon remove most oxygen from the atmosphere.

29. "Plankton" refers to organisms that float on water and do not swim.

30. Nitrogen does not play well with most other elements—that is, it doesn't react with them chemically—which is why it is so abundant in the atmosphere. Algae and some bacteria are able to extract nitrogen (N_2) from the air and convert it into ammonia (NH_3), which plants use to make nitrates. This process of extracting nitrogen and converting it into ammonia is called "fixing" nitrogen.

31. Mercury's surface temperature can vary by more than 1,000° F between the side facing the Sun and the side facing away. The Moon's sunny side can be 500° F hotter than its dark side. Temperatures on Mars can vary as much as 300° F.

32. Earth's atmospheric pressure is 14.7 pounds per square inch at sea level.

33. The vast majority of climate scientists believe we are sabotaging the carbon cycle by injecting large amounts of carbon dioxide into the atmosphere through the burning of fossil fuels and the destruction of tropical rain forests. You can read more about that in Chapter Eleven of my book, *Beyond Blind Faith: Reasons for the Hope We Have (1 Peter 3:15)*, entitled "Apocalypse Soon."

34. Plate tectonics is also called continental drift.

35. Among the planets and moons in our solar system, only Earth appears to have plate tectonics.

36. This has in fact happened to the other three terrestrial planets in the solar system—Mercury, Venus, and Mars—all of which lack a large moon. (Mars has two tiny moons, each less than seven miles in diameter.) The angle of tilt in their rotation has varied considerably.

37. The Moon's orbit is slowly expanding, so eventually the Moon will move far enough from Earth to lose its impact. But that will not happen

in my lifetime or yours, because the Moon is moving away at a rate of only four centimeters per year. At that rate, the Moon will continue to affect the Earth for at least several hundred-thousand years, and probably longer.

38. A substance's specific heat is the amount of energy needed to raise the temperature of one gram of that substance by one degree Centigrade.

39. All organisms are mostly water—sixty to seventy percent for humans.

40. Salt and sugar are examples of substances that will dissolve in water. Oil will not.

41. The pH scale ranges from one to fourteen. A pH of six or less is acidic, while a pH of eight or more is alkaline. The scale is exponential rather than linear, so each whole number on the scale represents a change in pH by a factor of ten. Thus, a substance with a pH of 3 is 100 times more acidic than a substance with a pH of 5, and 1,000 times more acidic than a substance with a pH of 6. Water has a pH of seven.

42. Stomach acid is highly acidic, with a pH of one to two. The acid is so destructive that stomach cells have to be continuously replaced every couple of weeks. The pancreas releases a strong base (i.e., alkaline) to neutralize this acid when food passes into the small intestine.

43. For example, the pH in our cells is 6.8, and the pH is our blood is 7.4. Neutral pH is 7.0.

44. However, some organisms rely on other sources of energy, such as chemicals in deep ocean vents.

Chapter 15
Making Sense of the Resurrection Stories

The authors of the New Testament agree that Jesus was crucified by the Romans and raised from death several days later. Yet the stories they tell about his post-resurrection appearances seem, at first glance, confusing and even conflicting. In Luke and Acts, everything occurs in or near Jerusalem, but Matthew and John describe events in Galilee as well. What we have of Mark's original gospel stops at Mark 16:8, before the risen Jesus even appears.[1] We also have a brief passage in 1 Corinthians in which Paul recounts what he learned about Jesus' resurrection appearances.

Mark was probably not an eyewitness to any of these events. Early Christian writers say that he was Peter's interpreter and based his gospel on what he heard Peter say. Luke and Paul were certainly not eyewitnesses, since they came to the faith well after Jesus' ascension. Luke and Paul both candidly admitted that they were reporting what people had told them—in Luke's case, after "having investigated everything carefully from the beginning." (Luke 1:3)[2]

The author of John's gospel tells us that he was an eyewitness,[3] and early Christian writers say that the gospels of Matthew and John were written by the two apostles who bore those names. If true, then both were eyewitnesses to some, but not all, of what they describe. Even those two apostles had to rely on other witnesses' accounts for some details, such as what the women discovered at the empty tomb.

Chapter 15 – Making Sense of the Resurrection Stories

The purpose of this chapter is to reconcile these different accounts and set forth what actually happened—at least as far as we can determine. As we do so, please keep in mind that different people perceive events differently, depending upon their perspective and their unconscious biases, and when they recount what occurred they often remember or emphasize different aspects of the event. If you doubt this, just listen to a Democrat, a Republican, and an Independent describe the same political event, or the same politician.

As I stated in the Preface, my starting point in biblical interpretation is that the New Testament writers were honestly reporting what they knew or believed to be true. But to find the truth, we must be prepared to piece together their different accounts, much like the testimony of witnesses in a courtroom, each of whom knows or tells only a portion of the whole.

I will first set forth a summary of what I believe actually happened, and then I will explain how I arrived at my conclusions.

What I Believe Happened

The Women. Jesus was crucified on a Wednesday, a Thursday, or a Friday—there are good arguments for each based on scripture,[4] but they are beyond the scope of this chapter. He rose from the dead sometime between Saturday evening and the early morning hours of Sunday. During this time, most of his followers—who were in or near Jerusalem—were laying low, afraid that they might be arrested by the Jewish authorities because of their association with Jesus. These followers included Jesus' eleven remaining apostles—

all but Judas Iscariot, who had committed suicide[5]—and others.

Before dawn on Sunday, several of Jesus' female disciples set out from either Jerusalem or Bethany to visit the tomb, bringing spices to anoint his corpse. Traveling as a group for safety reasons, these women included Mary Magdalene, Salome and Joanna (who might be the same person), Mary the mother of James,[6] and several others. They reached the tomb around dawn and were startled to see that the stone sealing the tomb had been rolled away. The soldiers guarding the tomb[7] had already fled. Nearby the women saw what appeared to be two young men in white robes, whom the disciples later realized must have been angels.

One of the young men spoke to the women, telling them that Jesus had risen. The young man instructed them to report this to the other disciples and to tell them that they were to go to Galilee, where they would see Jesus again. Frightened, the women hurried back and made their report. Not surprisingly, the men dismissed the story about the young men as nonsense—maybe the result of an overactive imagination or someone's cruel joke. Yet the men wondered about the empty tomb—could the women have gone to the wrong tomb?

Peter, John, and Jesus. Peter and John ran to the tomb to check it out. John, the younger of the two, ran faster and reached the tomb first but was afraid to actually go inside. Peter, the bold apostle who had tried to walk on water, arrived and entered the tomb, where he saw the linen wrappings and face cloth that had been on Jesus' body. But the body was gone. That made no sense. Who would bother to unwrap the body before stealing it?

Chapter 15 – Making Sense of the Resurrection Stories

Seeing that the tomb was safe, John followed Peter inside and realized that the women's report about the disappearance of Jesus' body was true. Bewildered by what it might mean, Peter and John returned to the rest of the disciples.

The women, including Mary Magdalene, had followed Peter and John, but they either lagged behind or waited at a discreet distance while the men examined the tomb. When they left, the women remained. Perhaps they needed to rest after making several trips already, or maybe they were still too distraught to leave. They must have doubted the reliability of what the angels had said, for they were far from joyful. Mary, at least, was sobbing. The women needed more convincing. So the angels returned.

When Mary Magdalene looked in the tomb, she saw the two angels again, one of whom asked her why she was crying. She responded that someone had taken her "Lord"—i.e., his body—and she did not know where they had taken him.

Then a man came up behind her and asked her why she was crying. Believing him to be the gardener, she assumed that he had moved Jesus' body—perhaps to bury it somewhere else. So she asked him where the body was so she (or someone) could take possession of it. When the man called her by name, Mary immediately recognized Jesus and fell at his feet. He told her to go to his disciples and tell them that she had seen him, that he would soon ascend to the Father, and that they were to meet him in Galilee.

Mary reported all of this to the disciples, but again they did not believe her. They were certain her story could not possibly be true. And they weren't going to leave the safety of their sanctuary in Jerusalem and risk the journey to Galilee on the word of Mary or any of the other women.

Emmaus and Jerusalem. To get the disciples to leave Jerusalem and go to Galilee, Jesus needed to convince them that he was really alive, so he made three more appearances that Sunday.

The first appearance was to Cleopas and an unnamed companion, who had left Jerusalem that morning. They were traveling to Emmaus, a quiet village about seven miles away. Before leaving, they had heard the women's initial story, as well as Peter's report about the empty tomb, but they were gone before Mary reported seeing Jesus alive.

Along the way to Emmaus the two disciples met a man who seemed unaware of Jesus' crucifixion and the empty tomb. But the man knew the Scriptures. As they walked, he explained how the Old Testament prophecies about the Messiah—"Christ" in Greek—demonstrated that he had to suffer and die before attaining glory.

When the three reached Emmaus, Cleopas invited this stranger to stay and eat with them. He agreed, but vanished after he broke bread and gave it to them. They suddenly realized that they had been talking with Jesus. So they hurried back to Jerusalem to tell his disciples, and learned that Jesus had by then also appeared to Peter.

As the disciples discussed these events Jesus appeared again, this time in their midst. He spoke to them, showed them the wounds in his hands and feet, and even ate some fish to prove that he was not a ghost. He instructed them to go to Galilee, as the angels had told the women. But Thomas was not present, and he refused to go anywhere on the word of what seemed like a bunch of crazy people. Unwilling to leave Thomas alone, and perhaps beginning to doubt their eyes or their sanity, they remained in Jerusalem.

Eight days later, Jesus appeared among his followers again. This time Thomas was there. Seeing Jesus alive with his own eyes, Thomas accepted the truth of the resurrection.

Galilee. Finally united in their conviction that Jesus was indeed alive, the disciples left Jerusalem and traveled north to Galilee. Probably staying in or near Peter's hometown of Capernaum, they waited. But Jesus did not immediately appear, and they grew bored. So Peter, John, James, Thomas, Nathanael, and two others went fishing. All night. They caught nothing.

At dawn, they saw a man on the shoreline who had built a fire. When they informed him that they had caught no fish, he told them to try again, this time on the right side of the boat. The resulting catch of fish was so great that it strained both the nets and the fishermen. John realized that this man was Jesus. Upon hearing John say so, Peter jumped in the water and swam to shore while the others brought in the catch of fish.

After breakfast, Jesus spoke with Peter, asking him three times, "Do you love Me?" Each time Peter responded affirmatively, after which Jesus told him to take care of Jesus' "sheep"—meaning, of course, people. Jesus then predicted Peter's martyrdom, saying, "when you grow old, you will stretch out your hands and someone else will gird you, and bring you where you do not wish to go." (John 21:18)[8] Peter saw John nearby and asked, "What about him?" Jesus responded, "If I want him to remain until I come, what *is that* to you? You follow Me!" (John 21:21-22) Some misinterpreted this comment to mean that John would never die.[9]

In the days that followed, Jesus led his disciples away from the villages of Galilee to a nearby mountain where they could be by themselves. There he taught them what they would need to know to carry on after his ascension. Word about his resurrection spread among his followers and more than 500 came to see the risen Jesus for themselves. Yet despite what their eyes told them, some still wondered, "Can this really be true?" During this time in Galilee he also showed himself to his mother Mary, his brother James, and his other brothers, who became his followers.[10]

The Great Commission and the Ascension. The time for the Jewish Feast of Weeks approached. This was one of three annual festivals which required Jews to return to Jerusalem to worship God. This religious celebration, also known as Pentecost, was about seven weeks after Passover. Knowing that it would draw large crowds, Jesus directed his disciples to return to Jerusalem. But before they left, he gave them the Great Commission:

> Go therefore and make disciples of all the nations, baptizing them in the name of the Father and the Son and the Holy Spirit, teaching them to observe all that I commanded you; and lo, I am with you always, even to the end of the age.
>
> —Matthew 28:19-20

Jesus met them in Jerusalem and instructed them to remain in the city until they received power from the Holy Spirit. Then he led them to nearby Bethany, where he blessed them and ascended into heaven. After he was gone, two angels in white appeared and told the disciples that Jesus would one day return "in just the same way as you have watched Him go into heaven." (Act 1:11)

How I Got There

The Women at the Tomb. The stories about Jesus' resurrection are found in six books of the New Testament:

Matthew 28:1-20
Mark 16:1-8
Luke 24:1-53
John 20:1-31 and 21:1-25
Acts 1:1-11
1 Corinthians 15:3-8

Each of the four gospels begins on the Sunday morning after Jesus' crucifixion, when some women went to the tomb in which his body had been laid a few days earlier by Joseph of Arimathea.[11] Early on we encounter our first discrepancy—exactly when did the women go? The four gospel writers differ only slightly:

Matthew 28:1: "as it began to dawn"
Mark 16:2: "Very early . . . when the sun had risen"
Luke 24:1: "at early dawn"
John 20:1: "early . . . while it was still dark"

We can easily resolve this minor discrepancy if we consider that the tomb was located outside the city of Jerusalem, and the women were on foot. They may have even traveled from Bethany—the home of Lazarus, Mary, Martha, and Simon the leper—where Jesus often stayed when he came to Jerusalem.[12] Bethany was a mile and three-quarters from Jerusalem,[13] so it would have been at least a thirty-minute walk each way. The women probably began their walk to the tomb while it was still dark, perhaps hoping to go unnoticed by the residents of the city, and arrived shortly after the sun had dawned.

The women came to the tomb expecting to find Jesus' body. Mark and Luke tell us that the women brought spices, and Mark clarifies that they had come to anoint the body.[14] The four gospels identify the women as:

Matthew 28:1: Mary Magdalene and "the other Mary"

Mark 16:1: Mary Magdalene, Mary the mother of James, and Salome

Luke 24:10: Mary Magdalene, Mary the mother of James, Joanna, and "other women"

John 20:1: Mary Magdalene

Thus, all four gospels agree that Mary Magdalene was there, and the three synoptic gospels—Matthew, Mark, and Luke—agree that Mary the mother of James accompanied her. Common sense would dictate that Mary Magdalene would not have walked to the tomb in the dark by herself. From the accounts of Mark and Luke we can be certain that at least two other women went with her, and Luke says there were more. Five or more probably made the trip because the women would have felt safer in a large group. The failure of Matthew and John to mention other women simply means that the writers did not consider the other women important to the story.

The Angels. When the women reached the tomb, they found it already opened—that is, the stone which had blocked the entrance had been rolled away.[15] Matthew explains that "a severe earthquake had occurred," and that an angel had rolled away the stone—events that apparently happened before the women arrived, but which had been witnessed by the guards who were watching the tomb. (Matthew 28:2-4)

Here we encounter our next discrepancy: who spoke to the women, and what was said? Mark says that "a young man" wearing a white robe told them that Jesus had risen, and instructed the women to tell his disciples "and Peter" to go to Galilee, where Jesus would meet them. (Mark 16:5-7) Matthew's account is substantially the same, except that he puts those words in the mouth of an angel dressed in "clothing as white as snow," rather than a man. (Matthew 28:5-7) In Luke, there are two men "in dazzling clothing" who deliver a similar message, although they do not mention going to Galilee. (Luke 24:3-7)

These three accounts are similar enough that they must be describing the same event. The women undoubtedly saw what they perceived to be two young men dressed in white, one of whom spoke to them. Sometime later, the disciples realized those "men" must have been angels, so that is how Matthew described them. Mark and Luke recorded the women's initial impression that these were just men. Mark and Matthew did not mention the second angel because he did not speak and made little impression on the women, but Luke's careful investigation[16] disclosed the memory of the second angel.

John is the outlier here. He does not mention the angels at this point in the story. He merely says that Mary Magdalene saw the stone rolled away from the tomb, so she ran and told Peter and "the other disciple whom Jesus loved"—presumably John—what she had seen. (John 20:1-2)

Peter and John both ran to the tomb to verify Mary's story. John, being the younger man, ran faster and reached the tomb first, but did not go in. When Peter caught up, he entered the tomb and saw that Jesus' body was gone. John followed Peter into the tomb, "and he saw and believed." (John 20:8) John and Peter then returned home, leaving Mary still at the empty tomb.

This is when John brings the angels into the story. Mary looked in the tomb, presumably reassured that it presented no danger in light of the investigation by Peter and John, and saw two angels in white. (John 20:11-12) The angels asked her why she was weeping, and she replied, "Because they have taken away my Lord, and I do not know where they have laid Him." (John 20:13)

Note that John does not explicitly contradict the other three gospels. He does not say that no angels appeared to Mary Magdalene when she first arrived at the tomb. He simply does not mention them.

If this seems odd, remember that the gospel writers were not historians, or even theologians. The gospels did not result from police interrogations or courtroom testimony. These were simple men who wrote what they believed was important for people of their own time to know. They never imagined that their words would be examined and scrutinized by people assessing their credibility two-thousand years after the fact. With that in mind, let's consider John's gospel.

John's was the last gospel to be written, perhaps about 90 A.D. The other three gospels were written between about 60 and 80 A.D., so they had already been circulating for many years. John may have read them and even discussed them with the original authors. Perhaps he did not repeat the story of the angels' initial appearance to the women because it was already common knowledge, having been covered by the other three gospel writers. Or maybe he simply believed they were unimportant at that point in the story. He wanted to focus on Mary Magdalene, since she was the first person to see Jesus alive again.

Another possibility is that Mary Magdalene did not see the angels' first appearance. She might have lagged behind the other women and missed it. If Mary was John's source for these events (remember John and the other men were not there yet) and Mary did not see the angels' initial visit, that could explain why John omits it. If this is what happened, then Mary Magdalene would have learned about the angels from the other women, seen the stone rolled away, and fled the scene with them so they could report it to the disciples.

The Women's Report. We will return to John's account shortly, but first we must address a potential discrepancy in Mark's gospel. Matthew, Luke, and John all say that the women hurried to tell the disciples about the empty tomb and what they had seen.[17] But Mark says: "They went out and fled from the tomb, for trembling and astonishment had gripped them; **and they said nothing to anyone**, for they were afraid." (Mark 16:8, emphasis added in boldface) Although Mark seems to be contradicting the other gospel writers, that is not really the case.

In Mark 1:40-45, he tells a story about Jesus healing a leper. After Jesus heals him, he tells the man: "See that you say nothing to anyone; but go, show yourself to the priest and offer for your cleansing what Moses commanded, as a testimony to them." (Mark 1:44) This verse means that Jesus told the man to go straight to the priest, without stopping to talk to anyone else along the way. Mark's use of a similar phrase in Mark 16:8 has a similar meaning.

In addition, Michael Licona—author of the extensively researched book, *The Resurrection of Jesus*—points out that the Greek word which Mark uses for "afraid" is the same word he uses on several other occasions to refer to the reverential fear people feel when they have an encounter with the divine.[18]

So Mark's account means that the women were so filled with awe that they went immediately to the disciples to report their encounter at the tomb, without talking to anyone else on the way.

Peter and John. Returning to John's gospel, his report about Peter's actions when he received the women's report is corroborated by Luke, who says that Peter ran to the tomb, looked inside, saw that the body was gone, and then returned home.[19] And according to Mark, the women were specifically instructed to tell Jesus' disciples "and Peter." (Mark 16:7) Obviously, they did.

John's gospel contains another apparent anomaly when Peter and John are at the tomb. After Peter entered the tomb, John followed. Then the writer adds: "and he [John] saw and believed." (John 20:8) Yet the verse which immediately follows seems to contradict this: "For as yet they did not understand the Scripture, that He must rise again from the dead." (John 20:9) What did John "believe" if he still did not understand that Jesus must rise again from the dead?[20]

The key to unraveling this mystery is in Luke's gospel. Right after the women's report about what they had seen and heard at the tomb, Luke tells us: "But these words appeared to them [the disciples] as nonsense, and they would not believe them." (Luke 24:11) The women had reported that the heavy stone had been rolled away and that the tomb was empty, but the men did not believe it. It must have seemed incredible. Why would anyone open the tomb and steal Jesus' body? Perhaps the men thought the women had gone to the wrong tomb.

So Peter and John ran to check it out and found the stone rolled away and the tomb empty, exactly as the women had said. What Peter and John believed at that point was the women's report that the tomb was indeed empty. They did not yet understand that Jesus had risen and was alive.

Jesus' First Appearance. After the men left and Mary Magdalene had seen the angels, John's gospel tells us that she turned around and saw someone she presumed was the gardener. So she asked him to tell her where Jesus' body was.[21] He replied by calling her by name. Then she recognized that the man was Jesus.[22] He gave her a message to take to the disciples—that "I ascend to My Father and your Father, and My God and your God." (John 20:17) Mary went to the disciples and reported seeing Jesus and what he had said.[23]

Matthew tells a similar story. After the angels had appeared to the women, Matthew 28:8-10 says:

> And they left the tomb quickly with fear and great joy and ran to report it to His disciples. And behold, Jesus met them and greeted them. And they came up and took hold of His feet and worshiped Him. Then Jesus said to them, "Do not be afraid; go and take word to My brethren to leave for Galilee, and there they will see Me."

Like the earlier appearance of the angels, Matthew indicates that several women were present, while John mentions only Mary Magdalene. This is not a contradiction, but merely a difference in emphasis. Since Jesus focuses on Mary, John does the same.

Meanwhile, the exact timing of this appearance in Matthew is not clear—was it before the women had made their report to the disciples, or after? John's gospel, however, clarifies this timing issue. He says it happened after the women reported to the disciples, and after Peter and John had run to the tomb and returned.

Thus, a gap in time occurs between Matthew 28:1-7 and 28:9-10. The former describes the angels' initial appearance, while the latter matches the angels' later appearance. Matthew 28:8 might fit with either one, depending on whether the verse is interpreted to refer to the women's first report (the empty tomb) or their second report (Jesus' appearance).

Jesus' Subsequent Appearances In and Near Jerusalem. What follows in John 20:19-25 is an appearance by Jesus to a group of disciples that does not include the apostle Thomas. This occurred in the "evening on that day, the first *day* of the week." (John 20:19) Jesus wished them peace, showed them his hands and his side to convince them that he had truly risen from the dead, and gave them a few further instructions.[24] Eight days later, Jesus appeared to them again, this time with Thomas present—and Thomas finally acknowledged the truth of Jesus' resurrection.[25] Then in chapter 21, John describes events that occurred in Galilee, and he plainly states that these events happened "after these things" that occurred in chapter 20. (John 21:1)

Chapter 15 – Making Sense of the Resurrection Stories

The first of these two appearances—the one Thomas missed—is corroborated by Luke,[26] who precedes that appearance with the story of Cleopas and another disciple traveling from Jerusalem to Emmaus, a village about seven miles from Jerusalem.[27] Luke makes clear that these two disciples were quite familiar with the events that had happened earlier that day, for as they were walking with Jesus (whom they had not yet recognized) they told him:

> But also some women among us amazed us. When they were at the tomb early in the morning, and did not find His body, they came, saying that they had also seen a vision of angels who said that He was alive. Some of those who were with us went to the tomb and found it just exactly as the women also had said; but Him they did not see.
>
> —Luke 24:22-24

These verses corroborate both the first appearance of the angels to the women and the verification of the empty tomb by Peter and John. But Luke does not mention Jesus' appearance to Mary Magdalene. The obvious reason is that Cleopas and his companion left for Emmaus before Mary had returned the second time and reported seeing Jesus alive. This also confirms the gap in time between Matthew 28:1-7 and Matthew 28:9-10, because Cleopas knew about the former but not the latter.

Luke tells us that Jesus joined the two disciples along the road, but they did not recognize him. As they walked toward Emmaus, he explained how the Scriptures foretold that the Messiah had to suffer and die before entering into his glory. When they reached Emmaus, Jesus broke bread with them, then immediately vanished as soon as they recognized him. So the two disciples hurried back to Jerusalem to report what they had seen and heard to "the eleven and those who were with them." (Luke 24:33)

Although the angels had left instructions with the women that the disciples were to travel to Galilee, that is not where these two disciples were bound. Scholars believe Emmaus was west or northwest of Jerusalem, whereas the normal route to Galilee would have taken them east to the Jordan River and then north. In addition, if the two disciples had been traveling to Galilee, they could have continued on their way instead of returning to Jerusalem. They were not on their way to Galilee, of course, because they had not believed the women's report.[28] They went on with their lives — so Jesus had to intervene and redirect them.

Another detail in Luke's gospel is quite interesting. Cleopas' companion is not named. Perhaps he was traveling with his wife. But Luke 24:34 says that when they returned to Jerusalem Cleopas told the disciples, "The Lord has really risen and has appeared to Simon." Peter's Jewish name was Simon Barjona.[29] Jesus gave Simon the additional name of Peter — or Cephas, which is the Aramaic version — meaning "rock," perhaps to distinguish him from Simon the Zealot, another of Jesus' twelve apostles.[30]

Could Peter have been Cleopas' companion? One objection to this possibility is that Cleopas and his companion reported to "the eleven and those who were with them" (Luke 24:33), which would ordinarily include Peter as one of "the eleven." Yet we know from John's gospel that Thomas was not there. So "the eleven" appears to be a generic reference to Jesus' inner circle of followers — those whom Matthew called "the twelve apostles" before Judas' death. (Matthew 10:2)[31] 1 Corinthians 15:5 provides another example of the generic use of the term. There Paul says that Jesus appeared to "the twelve" at a time when only eleven of this inner circle remained alive—i.e., after Judas' death but before Matthias replaced him, which occurred after Jesus' ascension.[32] This objection is therefore not persuasive.

A much stronger objection is that the gospel writers, including Luke, consistently refer to Peter by name. Why should Luke be obscure about his identity in this single instance? Primarily for this reason, I do not believe Peter was the other disciple with Cleopas, although I concede that it is possible.

Yet Jesus must have appeared to Peter sometime prior to the appearance at which Thomas was absent. We know this not only from Luke 24:34, which says Jesus had previously appeared to "Simon," but also from what Paul says in his first letter to the Corinthians. In 1 Corinthians 15:5-8 Paul lists Jesus' post-resurrection manifestations in chronological order[33] (although he omits the women and Cleopas). First on Paul's list is "Cephas"—i.e., Peter—followed by "the twelve." The latter undoubtedly refers to the meeting which Thomas had missed. If Peter was not the companion of Cleopas, then Jesus must have come to Peter at a time and place not explicitly recorded in the gospels.

While Cleopas and his companion were making their report to the disciples, they all suddenly saw Jesus standing in their midst.[34] Luke's account of this first appearance to the gathered disciples closely parallels that of John. As in John's gospel, Jesus showed the disciples his hands and feet to prove that he had truly risen.[35] Luke adds that he ate some fish to demonstrate that he was not a ghost.[36]

Jesus in Galilee. What follows in Luke's gospel is, I believe, a significant gap in time. Luke 24:44 begins, "Now He said to them," followed by Jesus explaining the scriptures to them: the many prophecies that Jesus had fulfilled; the Messiah's suffering, death, and resurrection; and how repentance for forgiveness of sins must be proclaimed to all nations.[37] After this, according to Luke 24:49-51, Jesus tells them to remain in Jerusalem "until you are clothed with power from on high," then leads them to Bethany where he ascends into Heaven. Acts 1:4-9 is similar to Luke 24:49-51, but Acts 1:3 adds something important: "To these He also presented Himself alive after His suffering, by many convincing proofs, appearing to them over *a period of* forty days and speaking of the things concerning the kingdom of God."

Luke's gospel summarizes these forty days in just a few verses—i.e., Luke 24:44-48. But Matthew and John tell us about events that Luke skips: Jesus' return to Galilee.

Recall that the angels' original instructions were to tell the disciples to go to Galilee. The disciples did not obey those orders initially because they did not believe the women's story. Most of the disciples hunkered down in Jerusalem, afraid to venture out. So Jesus intervened, appearing to the two disciples along the road, then to Peter, and then twice in eight days to the group in Jerusalem.

Finally convinced that Jesus had truly risen from the dead, the disciples belatedly moved to the friendlier and safer environment of Galilee.[38] Here, away from the Jewish religious leaders and the Roman officials, Jesus could spend time teaching and preparing his followers to carry on after his approaching ascension.

The gospels mention two appearances by the risen Jesus in Galilee—one briefly described by Matthew and the other extensively discussed in John's gospel. In Matthew 28:16-20, Jesus appeared to his disciples on "the mountain which Jesus had designated."[39] There Jesus gave them the Great Commission, to

> Go therefore and make disciples of all the nations, baptizing them in the name of the Father and the Son and the Holy Spirit, teaching them to observe all that I commanded you; and lo, I am with you always, even to the end of the age.
>
> —Matthew 28:19-20

Matthew 28:17 adds that Jesus' disciples worshiped him there, "but some were doubtful." Michael Licona points out that the word translated "doubtful" is the same Greek word used in Matthew 14:30-31, the story about Peter walking on water, where Jesus asked Peter why he "doubted." The Greek word means to have conflicting thoughts, as in Mark 9:24: "I do believe; help my unbelief."[40] It would be like our saying, "I can't believe my eyes."

John's gospel tells the story of the disciples going fishing by the Sea of Tiberias (the Roman name for the Sea of Galilee), seeing and meeting Jesus on the beach, and Jesus' lengthy conversation with Peter.[41] John tells us that this was the third time Jesus had appeared to his disciples since his resurrection,[42] apparently ignoring the visits with Cleopas and with Peter because they were to individuals rather than in a group setting. Since John has already told us about the first two appearances—i.e., the one in Jerusalem without Thomas present and the second eight days later at which Thomas was present—this third appearance must have occurred before the Great Commission described by Matthew.

Galilee was almost certainly the location where Jesus "appeared to more than five-hundred brethren at one time," as well as to his brother James, both of which Paul mentions in 1 Corinthians 15:6-7. Galilee would have been the logical place for both of these appearances to occur, since that was where Jesus spent most of his ministry, where he gained his early popularity, where most of his followers probably lived, and where his family still lived.

After James, Paul tells us that Jesus appeared to "all the apostles."[43] What Paul means by "the apostles" is cloudy, but he cannot be referring to "the twelve"[44] since he already listed them in 1 Corinthians 15:5. The term, "apostle," is from the Greek, *apostolos*, which means "a person sent forth."[45] Paul uses the term for himself and others,[46] so he must mean people like himself who were sent by God to proclaim the gospel. Maybe Paul is referring to the people to whom Jesus directed the Great Commission, in order to distinguish them from those who became Jesus' followers after the Ascension and Pentecost.

During those forty days of Acts 1:3, Jesus spoke to his followers "of the things concerning the kingdom of God."[47] Most of those forty days were probably spent in the relative safety and tranquility of Galilee, where he could instruct them without being disturbed.

As those forty days neared an end, Jesus instructed his followers to return to Jerusalem, knowing the time of Pentecost was approaching. Pentecost was one of three annual week-long festivals during which all Jews were supposed to congregate in Jerusalem,[48] so Jesus knew large crowds would be present.

After the disciples returned to Jerusalem, Jesus told them to remain in the city until they received power through the baptism of the Holy Spirit.[49] That event occurred a few days later, during the Pentecost celebration, when about 3,000 people became Christians.[50]

After giving his followers these final instructions, Jesus led them to Bethany, where he ascended into Heaven.[51]

Endnotes for Chapter Fifteen, "Making Sense of the Resurrection Stories"

1. Mark 16:9-20 is not part of the earliest manuscripts we have of Mark's gospel. Assuming the original gospel contained something after Mark 16:8, those additional verses have been lost to history.

2. For Paul, see 1 Corinthians 15:3.

3. See John 21:24.

4. If you are interested, you can find arguments for all three possibilities on the internet.

5. Matthew 27:3-5

6. Mark and Luke do not identify which "James" they are referring to. The New Testament mentions four different individuals with that name:

> James the son of Zebedee and brother of John (aka James the Greater)
> James the brother of Jesus (aka James the Just)
> James the son of Alphaeus (aka James the Less)
> James the father of Judas, one of Jesus' twelve apostles

Based on Mark 15:40, the "Mary" referred to by Mark and Luke was probably the mother of James the Less, since Mark 15:40 tells us that this Mary was present at Jesus' crucifixion, along with Mary Magdalene and Salome. However, we cannot be certain.

7. The soldiers are mentioned only by Matthew, who does not make clear whether they were Roman soldiers or Jewish temple guards. The question is unimportant for our purposes.

8. Tradition says that Peter was crucified upside down in Rome in about 68 A.D.

9. John 21:23

10. Acts 1:14

11. See Matthew 27:57-60, Mark 15:42-46, Luke 50-53, and John 19:38-42.

12. See Matthew 21:17, 26:6; Mark 11:11-12, 14:3; John 11:1, 11:18, 12:1-3.

13. John 11:18 says that Bethany was about 15 *stadia*—about 9,090 feet—from Jerusalem. This would be about 1.72 miles.

14. Mark 16:1 and Luke 24:1

Chapter 15 – Making Sense of the Resurrection Stories

15. Matthew 28:2, Mark 16:4, Luke 24:2, and John 20:1

16. Luke 1:3

17. See Matthew 28:8, Luke 24:9, and John 20:2.

18. Licona, Michael R., *The Resurrection of Jesus*, p. 347

19. Luke 24:12

20. Some interpret these verses to mean that John believed Jesus had risen from the dead, but did not yet understand that his resurrection was in fulfillment of scripture. Yet this interpretation seems inconsistent with the disciples' subsequent behavior, such as the nonchalance of Peter and John after leaving the tomb (John 20:10), the disciples' persistent fear of the authorities (John 20:19), and their skepticism when Jesus finally appeared to them (Luke 24:37).

21. John 20:14-15

22. John 20:16. This was not the only time Jesus' disciples failed to recognize him. On the road to Emmaus, Cleopas and his companion walked a long way with Jesus without recognizing him. Peter, John, and other disciples did not recognize him when they saw him on the shoreline of the Sea of Galilee as they were fishing. The New Testament authors do not tell us why this was so. Perhaps Jesus' appearance had changed. Or maybe this is another example of the principle that we see what we expect to see—and no one expected to see Jesus alive again that Sunday morning.

23. John 20:18

24. John 20:19-23

25. John 20:24-29

26. The story of the two disciples on the road to Emmaus is in Luke 24:13-35.

27. Luke 24:13-33. Two older manuscripts indicate that Emmaus may have been as far as twenty miles from Jerusalem. Yet I doubt this because a forty-mile round trip seems too far to complete in one day.

28. Luke 24:11

29. See, for example, Matthew 4:18, 10:2, and 16:16-18; Mark 1:16; and John 1:40-42.

30. Matthew 10:4; Mark 3:18; Luke 6:15

31. See also Mark 3:16-19 and Luke 6:13-16.

32. Compare Acts 1:9 and 1:21-26.

33. Paul's phrasing makes clear that he is listing Jesus' appearances in order, because he uses the terms "then" and "after that," concluding the list with "and last of all."

34. Luke 24:36

35. Luke 24:39-40

36. Luke 24:37, 41-42

37. Luke 24:45-48

38. Matthew 28:16

39. Matthew 28:16

40. Licona, Michael R., *The Resurrection of Jesus*, pp. 358-362

41. See John 21:1-23.

42. John 21:14

43. 1 Corinthians 15:7

44. Jesus' twelve apostles were: Simon Peter, James son of Zebedee, his brother John, Peter's brother Andrew, Philip, Bartholomew, Thomas, Matthew, James son of Alphaeus, Thaddaeus (whom Luke calls Judas son of James), Simon the Zealot, and Judas Iscariot. See Matthew 10:2-4; Mark 3:16-19; and Luke 6:14-16.

45. *Webster's New World Dictionary*, p. 65

46. Paul calls himself an "apostle" in Romans 1:1 and 11:13; 1 Corinthians 1:1, 9:1-2, and 15:9; 2 Corinthians 1:1; Galatians 1:1; Ephesians 1:1; Colossians 1:1; 1 Thessalonians 2:6; 1 Timothy 1:1 and 2:7; 2 Timothy 1:1 and 1:11; and Titus 1:1. In addition, in Romans 16:7, he calls Andronicus and Junias apostles.

47. Acts 1:3

48. The other two annual feasts were the Feast of Unleavened Bread, which was immediately after Passover, and the Feast of Booths (also known as the Feast of Tabernacles or the Feast of the Ingathering). For

Chapter 15 – Making Sense of the Resurrection Stories

more, see Exodus 12:14-20, 23:15-16, 34:18, 34:22; Leviticus 23:6-21, 23:33-36, 23:39-44; Numbers 28:16-31, 29:12-39; and Deuteronomy 16:1-16.

49. See Luke 24:49 and Acts 1:4-5 and 1:8.

50. See Acts 2:1-41.

51. See Luke 50-51 and Acts 1:9.

Chapter 16
THE BIRTH OF JESUS
(Historical Fiction)

Preface

What we were taught as children about the birth of Jesus is probably not exactly the way it happened. I do not mean that the Bible story is wrong. However, that story has been misinterpreted, and sometimes interpolated, so that the Christmas story we so often see in church or on television is seriously flawed.

What follows is a fictional account crafted to be consistent with what scholars believe truly happened, given what we know about first century Israel and what the Gospels actually say. For example:

Time of Year. Although somewhat controversial, most scholars believe Jesus was born sometime in the fall, not in December.

"No room at the inn." Luke 2:7 uses the Greek word, *kataluma*, which means "guest room." Inns—as in Luke 10:34—were usually along trading routes and located in large towns. Bethlehem was neither. In addition, Eastern hospitality traditions would have precluded turning away a relative, or even a stranger, and especially one with a pregnant wife. Since Joseph's ancestors were from Bethlehem, he and Mary probably stayed with relatives there, at least until sometime after Jesus' birth.

Timing of the birth. Luke 2:6 implies that Joseph and Mary arrived in Bethlehem at least a few days before Jesus was born: "**While they were there**, the days were completed for her to give birth." (emphasis added via boldface)

Born in a Stable? The Bible does not actually say Jesus was born in a stable. It merely says he was laid in a manger, which is a feeding trough for animals. In first century Israel people often brought animals inside their homes at night for the safety of the animals and for the added warmth from their body heat. Thus, many first century Jewish homes had mangers inside.

The Birth of Jesus

A drop of sweat rolled down Hannah's forehead as she finished cleaning the animal pen that occupied one-quarter of the lower floor of her tiny house. The pen protected the most vulnerable of her animals at night, and they in turn provided needed heat on cold nights. During these warm Autumn days, Hannah normally cleaned the pen in the cool early morning hours. But today her duties toward her seven houseguests had kept her busy until almost mid-morning.

With the job at last finished, she sat down to rest, only to be disturbed by a loud knocking. Muttering, she dragged herself up and opened the door. A tall man with a dark beard filled the doorway. He wore a brown cloak over a beige wool tunic. A cloth held in place by a leather cord covered his head. She recognized him immediately.

"Joseph!" She jumped upon him and threw her arms around his neck, leaving her feet dangling a couple of inches off the floor. "Dear brother, where have you been?"

He wrapped his arms around his older sister's waist and effortlessly lifted her further off the ground, but said nothing. Then he gently set her down.

She cupped his face in her hands. "We were so worried. Daniel and Rachel arrived several days ago and said you were no more than a day's journey behind them."

"We're fine, Sis. Is Daniel here? I'd like to talk to him."

"No, he and Samuel went into town to ask if anyone had seen you."

The man moved aside to reveal a petite young woman standing behind him. "Hannah, this is my wife, Mary."

A huge grin burst across Hannah's face. "Mary," she squealed, and she hugged her sister-in-law like a long-lost friend, even though they had never met. Finally letting go, Hannah seized the young woman's hands and said, "Oh, let me look at you."

Mary seemed more girl than woman, perhaps about 15 or 16 years old, with some teenage acne and long, straight black hair emerging from underneath her head scarf. Her dark brown eyes revealed a maturity and intelligence that belied her youth. Although she wore a long, loose-fitting wool tunic that concealed most of the contours of her body, the large bulge near her stomach left no doubt that she would soon deliver her first child.

"Mary, Mary," Hannah began again, "you are as beautiful as Daniel said you are." The flattery elicited a shy smile from the girl. "But you must be exhausted, you poor dear. A curse be upon the Emperor for making you travel in your condition. Are you hungry? I have bread and some pomegranates."

The girl gently shook her head. "No, please, I just need to lie down for awhile."

"Of course you do, my dear. Come, come, let's find you a place to lie down. Can you climb a ladder?"

The girl nodded. "I think so."

The two of them walked over to a sturdy wooden ladder leaning against the house's upper floor, which was only half the size of the ground level. As Mary started to climb, Hannah looked back at Joseph. "Where are your belongings?"

He motioned toward the front door. "Still on our donkey. I left him outside."

"Well, unburden the poor beast and tie him up under one of the large shade trees while I take your wife upstairs. You can bring him inside tonight if you like."

He turned and walked outside.

Mary inched her way up the ladder, with Hannah following close behind to help steady her. Once they were upstairs, Hannah unrolled a mat for the girl to lie on. She was asleep before her sister-in-law had climbed back down.

Joseph returned and set two large sacks in a corner. Hannah gave him some bread, which he devoured. After he finished, she handed him a large pouch made of sheepskin. "Come, Joseph," she whispered, "you can help me draw water and tell me all about your trip." She picked up a large earthenware pitcher and placed it on her left shoulder, holding it steady with one hand.

"We left Nazareth almost two weeks ago," he said when they were outside, "a few days after we heard about the Emperor's edict. At first we traveled south with a group of pilgrims from Cana."

Hannah turned on Joseph. "You didn't go through Samaria, I hope."

"No, of course not," he said. "We went east through the Valley of Jezreel to the Jordan River valley."

As they walked the quarter mile to one of the community wells, he described their journey south along the road that parallels the Jordan River until they were overtaken by Daniel and Rachel near Alexandrium.

"Where is Alexandrium?," she inquired.

"Near Mount Sartaba."

His sister gave him a playful slap on the arm with her free hand. "That's not helpful. You know I've never traveled far from Bethlehem."

Joseph suppressed a chuckle. "Of course. I'm sorry. Alexandrium is about a day's journey north of Jericho. Do you know where Jericho is?"

She gently slapped his arm again. "Of course I do. Don't be so mean."

"Then again," he went on, "it took us almost two days to go from there to Jericho because Mary needed to stop and rest so much."

As they drew water from the well—filling up the pouch, the pitcher, and themselves—he recounted the trip from Alexandrium to Jericho. They had traveled there with Daniel, Rachel, and their five children.

"What I don't understand," said Hannah as they started back to the house, "is why Daniel would leave you in Jericho, especially with your wife in her condition. I thought our cousin had more sense than that. Doesn't he know how dangerous that trip from Jericho to Jerusalem can be? There are robbers everywhere!"

"Actually, we insisted that they go on. We had already slowed them down enough. They had an opportunity to go with a group of pilgrims that were leaving that same day, and Mary was too tired to tackle the climb up to Jerusalem. We decided to wait and go with a group of merchants the next day. They even offered to let Mary ride in one of their carts. Let's stop here for a bit."

They stood in the shade of a large olive tree. Joseph wiped the sweat from his forehead, and gave Hannah a drink from the water pouch. As he took a drink himself, she looked up at him and asked, "If you left Jericho the day after Daniel, how did you fall so far behind?"

He wiped his mouth on his cloak and returned her gaze. "A terrible dust storm blew into Jericho the next morning and we had to wait until the weather cleared. Then a big thunderstorm erupted—"

"Yes," she interrupted, "it struck here, too."

"After that," he continued, "the roads were so muddy we ended up staying in Jericho two more days. We reached Jerusalem yesterday evening, and walked to Bethlehem this morning."

As they began walking again, Hannah said, "I'm glad you and Mary are safe. It's nice to have you both here."

When they got back to the house, Hannah set the pitcher down, then took the sheepskin pouch from Joseph and hung it from a nail in the wall. They both sat down on the floor, and she said, "We'll be out of the sun in here, but we'll need to talk quietly. Mary is resting."

He nodded his assent. "Of course."

Then she asked, "So what are your plans after you've registered for the census?"

He shook his head. "I'm not sure. I might like to stay through the winter. Anyway, we want to wait long enough to present Jesus at the Temple in Jerusalem—"

"Jesus?" she interrupted him, with a puzzled look on her face. "You mean the baby? What if it's a girl?"

"He's not a girl."

"You don't know that, Joseph."

"Yes, I do. The baby will be a boy, and we will name him Jesus." His voice had grown loud and insistent.

"Quiet!" she scolded him, her voice barely above a whisper. "Mary is trying to rest."

The tone of his voice immediately dropped as he said, "Oh yes, sorry."

Almost whispering, she said, "That sounds like wishful thinking, Joseph. How can you be so sure?"

He paused and looked up, as if he were contemplating the tiny house's flat ceiling. Hannah wondered if he was afraid to answer her question. Then he took one of her hands in his. "I know this may be hard to believe, Sis, but an angel told us."

She stared at him as if he had suddenly sprouted a camel hump, then covered her mouth with her free hand as she laughed.

"Quiet!" he scolded her, but with an amused look on his face, apparently enjoying the fact that he was able to return her earlier rebuke.

Stifling her laughter, she said, "An angel? My dear brother, you have either lost your mind or you are joking with me!"

"No, no, this is no joke," he insisted. Hannah saw from his stern expression that he was entirely serious. "An angel visited Mary and told her she was going to get pregnant and have a son, which she was to name Jesus."

"And you were there? You saw this angel?"

"Well, no," he admitted, "but after I found out she was pregnant, I was going to send her away. Then an angel appeared to me in a dream and told me the same thing. So I—"

She held up her hand to stop him. "Wait. Why were you going to send her away? She's your wife. Besides, if she was unfaithful she deserved to die according to the Law."

"Well, she wasn't my wife then. We were only betrothed. Anyway, the angel told me to go ahead and marry her, assuring me that she had not been unfaithful. The angel said the child was conceived by the Holy Spirit, and I was to name him Jesus."

"Wait. Are you saying Mary was a virgin when she got pregnant?"

"Yes. Actually, she still is."

Hannah sat in stunned silence for a few moments before saying, "People are going to think you're crazy, Joseph." Then she shrugged her shoulders, got to her feet, and retrieved a bowl filled with pomegranates. "But no matter, you're family. You're welcome to stay as long as you need to. Would you like a pomegranate?"

"Thanks, Sis," he said, taking one of the bright red fruits. "By the way, do you know anyone who needs a carpenter? If I'm going to stay for awhile, I'll need work."

She thought a moment. "Go see Aryeh. His family's rich and his wife just had twins. He's adding another room to his house and he needs a carpenter to help him finish the roof. You could do that, couldn't you?"

"Sure," Joseph mumbled through a mouthful of pomegranate.

"Terrific. Samuel can take you there tomorrow."

He swallowed and said, "I would be very grateful. I'll talk to him when he returns. By the way, where is Rachel? I need to let her know we arrived safely."

Hannah pointed toward the back of the house. "She and the children went out to the orchard to pick olives. Anything we don't eat tonight Samuel can sell in town tomorrow when he takes you to see Aryeh."

Standing up, still holding his pomegranate, Joseph said, "Then I'd better go help them."

A few minutes later, Hannah heard a sigh from the upper level of the house, followed by a soft voice that said, "Did Joseph leave?"

Hannah stood and walked to where she could see Mary leaning over the edge of the upper floor, looking down at her. "Yes, dear. He went out to pick fruit in the orchard. What do you need?"

Mary answered, "I would like to come down, but I'm not sure I can do it alone."

"That's all right, dear. I'll come help you."

Hannah met the girl at the ladder and helped her climb down. As they both sat on the floor, Hannah asked, "Would you like some bread now?"

"Yes, please."

Hannah handed her a piece of bread, then poured some water from the pitcher into a cup and gave it to the pregnant girl.

Between bites, and in a soft voice that Hannah could barely hear, Mary said, "Thank you. You are very kind."

Chapter 16 – The Birth of Jesus

"Not at all, dear. You're family now. I only wish we could offer you better sleeping quarters. Unfortunately, there's not much room upstairs, especially with Daniel and his family in the guest room. It's much too crowded for you and Joseph to fit in there. Samuel and I could try to make room for you with us, or you can sleep down here—but I warn you, Samuel is quite a snorer."

"Oh, down here will be fine. I'd prefer not to climb that ladder again, anyway."

"Of course." Hannah paused, gathering her courage to ask the question that was now dominating her thoughts. "Mary, Joseph told me a pretty wild story, about you being visited by an angel. Is that true?"

She nodded vigorously. "Oh yes. He told me that I would become pregnant and have a baby boy, and that I was to name him Jesus."

Hannah sighed. "I think you and Joseph better keep that to yourselves."

* * * *

A few days later, Mary woke up in the middle of the night. By the light of a nearly full moon shining through a window, she saw her husband sleeping on his back next to her, making noises that reminded her of a thunderstorm over the Sea of Galilee. She rolled toward him and touched his shoulder. "Joseph," she whispered.

He continued to snore.

She shook him, and her voice became louder and more insistent. "Joseph!"

He sat up and looked at her. "What's wrong?"

"The baby is coming."

Joseph rubbed his eyes. "Are you sure?"

"Of course I'm sure, you silly man. A woman knows these things."

Joseph stood up and called out, "Hannah!"

A woman's sleepy voice responded, "What's the matter, Joseph?"

"Mary is having the baby!"

With sudden urgency, the voice responded, "I'll be right down." Then the same voice called out, "Rachel! Get up! Mary is having her baby. I'm going to need your help. Samuel, wake up! Go get Anna, the midwife."

Soon the whole house was roused. Rachel lit two oil lamps, while Daniel and their children led the animals outside. Joseph started a fire to heat water, then joined Daniel. Samuel returned with Anna and several neighbors. The women went inside to help with the birth, while the men talked with Joseph.

Shortly before noon Hannah walked out to the orchard, where the men were sitting under some olive trees. The children were playing nearby.

"Joseph!" she called out as she came near.

He stood up and ran to her.

She beamed a radiant smile and let out a giggle of joy. "It's a boy, Joseph, just as you said. A fine, healthy boy."

"And Mary?"

"Also fine. You can go in now."

He ran to the house, pausing for only a few moments at the door to catch several deep breaths. Then he rushed inside. Hannah followed as quickly as she could. Once inside, she sat down next to Mary, who was lying on a mat. Rachel was standing nearby, holding the baby as she and Joseph cooed over him. The large man took the tiny child in his arms and kissed him. "Little Jesus," he whispered, remembering the words of the angel, "who will save his people from their sins."

Hannah looked up and said, "I'm sorry, what was that?"

Joseph winked at Mary before turning to address his sister. "I just said he looks sleepy. Do you have a place where he can sleep? We have no cradle."

Mary sat up on one elbow and pointed toward a corner of the animal pen. "What about over there? That would make a fine cradle."

Hannah looked to where Mary had pointed and cried out in disbelief, "The manger? You want to put him in a feeding trough?"

With some help from Rachel, Mary struggled to her feet and took the child from Joseph. "Yes, I think it would be perfect. He'll be quite comfortable, and we'll be close by if he needs us."

"Before you put him in there—," Rachel began, then looked at Joseph. "Do you have some clean cloths?"

"Of course," he said. He went to one of the sacks he had brought in and pulled out two small blankets.

Rachel took the blankets from him and handed them to Mary. "Wrap him up in these, nice and tight. He'll be a lot happier."

She did so, and then laid him gently in the manger.

Suddenly Samuel and Daniel rushed in.

"What is it?" Hannah growled at them, as if they had intruded on a secret meeting.

"Some shepherds," Samuel stammered. "Some shepherds are outside. They want to see the baby."

217

Standing up, she motioned him away with her hand. "Tell them to go away. They've no business here."

"But they say an angel sent them," Samuel retorted.

"Hannah." Mary's voice was gentle but insistent. "I think it'll be all right."

"Yes," Joseph echoed, "please send them in."

Samuel signaled for the shepherds to enter. All were quite young, with the oldest perhaps nineteen or twenty, and the youngest no more than thirteen. They immediately walked over to the manger, where they stared at the child.

Wrinkling her nose, Hannah whispered to her husband, "They stink, Samuel. Why did you let them in here?"

He only said, "Hush, wife."

The oldest shepherd turned toward Mary. "Are you his mother?" he asked.

"Yes," she replied. "Did you really see an angel?"

He nodded. "We were tending our sheep when the angel came and stood among us. We were scared to death, but he said, 'Don't be afraid. I bring you good news. Today in Bethlehem a Savior has been born, who is Christ the Lord.' And the angel told us what to look for—a baby wrapped in swaddling cloths and lying in a manger. We went to the house of Anna, the midwife, and her family told us we might find him here." Glancing back at the babe, he added, "And here he is."

Mary thanked him, and they soon left. But they could not contain their excitement, and by nightfall almost everyone in Bethlehem had heard the shepherds' tale.

BIBLIOGRAPHY

Adam Clarke's Commentary, in *Bible Explorer 4.0* software (WORDsearch 2006).

Alvarez, Walter. *T. rex and the Crater of Doom*. Princeton, NJ: Princeton University Press, 1997.

Baird, William, Cyril E. Blackman, James L. Price, Victor Paul Furnish, Leander E. Keck, and Eric Lane Titus, and ed. by Charles M. Laymon. *Interpreter's Concise Commentary: Acts & Paul's Letters*. Nashville: Abingdon Press, 1984.

Behe, Michael J. *The Edge of Evolution: The Search for the Limits of Darwinism*. New York: Free Press, 2007.

"Biology for Majors I; Module 2: The Chemistry of Life; The pH Scale," found at https://courses/lumenlearning.com/suny-wmopen-biology1/chapter/the-ph-scale/ (last viewed July 15, 2018).

"Blaise Pascal Biography," found at https://www.biography.com/people/blaise-pascal-9434176 (last viewed 4/3/2018).

Bucknell University, "Plate Tectonics," found at https://www.bucknell.edu/academics/arts-and-sciences-college-of/academic-departments-and-programs/geology-and-environmental-geosciences/location/geologic-history-of-central-pennsylvania/plate-tectonics, 2017 (last viewed November 5, 2018).

Cain, Fraser. "Composition of the Earth's Atmosphere," found at https://www.universetoday.com/26656/composition-of-the-earths-atmosphere/, March 9, 2009, updated December 24, 2015 (last viewed June 19, 2018).

Canales, Manuel, Matthew W. Chwastyk, and Eve Conant. "One Strange Rock: 6 Things That Make Life On Earth Possible," NationalGeographic.com web site, found at https://www.nationalgeographic.com/magazine/2018/03/one-strange-rock-interactive-earth-solar-system-milky-way-galaxy/ (last viewed 5/10/2018).

Canright, Shelley, ed. "Ozone: What is it, and why do we care about it?," found at https://www.nasa.gov/audience/foreducators/postsecondary/features/F_Ozone.html, last updated April 10, 2009 (last viewed June 15, 2018).

"Carbon Cycle and Earth's Climate, The," found at http://www.columbia.edu/~vjd1/carbon.htm (last viewed July 10, 2018).

Carlowicz, Michael. "NASA – New Simulation Shows Consequences of a World Without Earth's Natural Sunscreen," found at https://nasa.gov/topics/earth/features/world_avoided.html, March 18, 2009 (last viewed June 16, 2018).

Cham, Jorge, and Daniel Whiteson. *We Have No Idea: A Guide to the Unknown Universe*. New York: Riverhead Books, an imprint of Penguin Random House, 2017.

"Chapter 3: The Chemical Basis for Life; Lesson 1: The Unique Properties of Water," found at https://nanopdf.com/download/lesson-1-unique-properties-of-water_pdf (last viewed July 18, 2018).

Chawla, Anuj and Professor A.K. Lavania. "Oxygen Toxicity," found at

https://www.ncbi.nlm.nih.gov/pmc/articles/PMC4925
834/, July 21, 2011 (last viewed June 19, 2018).

Choi, Charles Q. "What Makes Earth So Perfect For Life?,"
October 18, 2012, found at
https://www.livescience.com/31788-why-earth-
perfect-for-life.html (last viewed May 10, 2018).

Dawood, N.J., translator. *The Koran*. London: Penguin Books,
1999.

De Pree, Christopher, Ph.D., and Alan Axelrod, Ph.D. *The
Complete Idiot's Guide to Astronomy* (4th Ed.). New
York: Alpha Books, a division of Penguin Group
(USA), 2008.

Dove, Laurie L. "What if the ozone layer disappeared?,"
found at https://science.howstuffworks.com/science-
vs-myth/what-if/what-if-ozone-layer-
disappeared.htm (last viewed June 16, 2018).

EarthSky. "Tunguska explosion," found at
http://earthsky.org/space/what-is-the-tunguska-
explosion, June 30, 2017 (last viewed June 28, 2018).

———. "What's a safe distance between us and a supernova?," found at http://earthsky.org/astronomy-
essentials/supernove-distance, May 11, 2018 (last viewed
July 9, 2018).

Fecht, Sarah. "What would happen if Earth started to spin
faster?," found at https://www.popsci.com/earth-spin-
faster, May 17, 2017 (last viewed July 15, 2018).

Gordon, Nicole. "Nitrogen in the Earth System," UCAR Center for Science Education, found at
https://www2.ucar.edu/news/backgrounders/nitrogen
-earth-system, last updated March 2015 (last viewed
June 19, 2018).

Guralnik, David B., ed. *Webster's New World Dictionary of the American Language, 2nd College Edition*. New York: Simon and Schuster, 1984.

Henry, Matthew. *Matthew Henry's Commentary on the Whole Bible*. Edited by Rev. Leslie F. Church, Ph.D., F.R.Hist.S. Grand Rapids, Michigan: Regency Reference Library, Zondervan Publishing House, 1961.

Hogenboom, Melissa. "BBC Earth: In Siberia in 1908, a huge explosion came out of nowhere," found at http://www.bbc.com/earth/story/20160706-in-siberia-in-1908-a-huge-explosion-came-out-of-nowhere, July 7, 2016 (last viewed June 28, 2018).

Israel, Brett. "New Study Describes How Earth's Surface Moves," found at https://www.livescience.com/29586-new-study-describes-how-earths-surface-moves.html, July 19, 2010 (last viewed July 14, 2018).

Jamieson-Fausset-Brown Bible Commentary, in *Bible Explorer 4.0* software, WORDsearch, 2006.

Lamb, Michael E., ed. *The Role of the Father in Child Development, 4th Edition*. New York: John Wiley & Sons, 2004.

Learn Astronomy HQ. "15 'Goldilocks' Factors That Allow Life on Earth to Exist," found at http://www.learnastronomyhq.com/articles/15-goldilocks-factors-that-allow-life-on-earth-to-exist.html (last viewed May 10, 2018).

Licona, Michael R. *The Resurrection of Jesus: A New Historiographical Approach*. Downers Grove, Illinois: InterVarsity Press, 2010.

The Life Application Concise New Testament Commentary, in *Bible Explorer 3.0* software, WORDsearch.

Luntz, Stephen. "The Speed of Light Can Vary in a Vacuum," January 21, 2015, found at http://www.iflscience.com/physics/speed-light-can-vary-vacuum (last viewed May 29, 2018).

Mays, James L., general ed. *Harper's Bible Commentary*. San Francisco: Harper & Row, 1988.

McGann, Chris. "What Is the Effect of PH on Living Organisms?," found at https://sciencing.com/effect-ph-living-organisms-6723807.html, last updated May 16, 2018 (last viewed July 15, 2018).

Miller, Steve. *The Complete Idiot's Guide to the Science of Everything*. New York: Alpha Books, a Member of Penguin Group (USA), Inc., 2008.

National Aeronautics and Space Administration (NASA). "Comets," found at https://solarsystem.nasa.gov/small-bodies/comets/in-depth/, updated December 7, 2017 (last viewed June 20, 2018).

———. "Earth's Atmospheric Layers," found at https://www.nasa.gov/mission_pages/sunearth/science/atmosphere-layers2.html, January 22, 2013 (last viewed June 28, 2018).

National Geographic. "Plate Tectonics Information and Facts," found at https://www.nationalgeographic.com/science/earth/the-dynamic-earth/plate-tectonics/ (last viewed July 15, 2018).

———. "Six Things That Make Life on Earth Possible," found at https://www.nationalgeographic.com/magazine/2018/

03/one-strange-rock-interactive-earth-solar-system-milky-way-galaxy/ (last viewed May 10, 2018).

"Pascal's Wager," Stanford Encyclopedia of Philosophy, found at https://plato.stanford.edu/entries/pascal-wager/ (last viewed 4/3/2018).

Pfeiffer, Charles F., and Everett F. Harrison, eds. *The Wycliffe Bible Commentary*. Chicago: Moody Press, 1962.

Quizlet. "Properties of Water That Make Life on Earth Possible," found at https://www.quizlet.com/208239239/properties-of-water-that-make-life-on-earth-possible-flash-cards/ (last viewed May 10, 2018).

Redd, Nola Taylor. "How Fast Does Light Travel?: The Speed of Light," March 6, 2018, found at http://www.space.com/15830-light-speed.html (last viewed May 29, 2018).

Rees, Martin. *Our Cosmic Habitat*. Princeton, NJ: Princeton University Press, 2001.

Rubin, Dr. Ken. "Abundance of Nitrogen in Earth's Atmosphere," found at https://www.soest.hawaii.edu/GG/ASK/atmo-nitrogen.html (last viewed June 19, 2018).

Ryden, Professor Barbara. "Lecture 31: The Center of Our Galaxy," found at http://www.astronomy.ohio-state.edu/~ryden/ast162_7/notes31.html (last viewed May 29, 2018).

Ryrie, Charles Caldwell, Th.D., Ph.D. *The Ryrie Study Bible: New American Standard Translation*, with annotations. Chicago: Moody Press, 1978.

Sagan, Carl. *Cosmos*. New York: Random House, 1980.

Science Pal. "Water and pH," found at
https://sites.google.com/a/bvsd.org/science-pal/biology/biochemistry/water-and-ph (last viewed July 15, 2018).

Sharp, Tim. "Earth's Atmosphere: Composition, Climate & Weather," found at http://www.space.com/17683-earth-atmosphere.html, October 13, 2017 (last viewed June 19, 2018).

Spence, Pam, ed. *The Universe Revealed*. New York: Cambridge University Press, 1998.

Stern, Victoria. "The Oxygen Dilemma: Can Too Much O_2 Kill?," found at https://www.scientificamerican.com/article/the-oxygen-dilemma/, October 1, 2008 (last viewed June 19, 2018).

Stierwalt, Sabrina. "What if the Earth rotated twice as fast?," found at http://curious.astro.cornell.edu/about-us/36-our-solar-system/the-earth/general-questions/17-what-if-the-earth-rotated-twice-as-fast-beginner, last updated June 27, 2015 (last viewed July 15, 2018).

Trefil, James. *1001 Things Everyone Should Know About Science*. New York: Doubleday, 1992.

UCAR Center for Science Education. "Earth's Atmosphere," found at https://scied.ucar.edu/shortcontent/earths-atmosphere, 2015 (last viewed June 19, 2018).

Ward, Peter D., and Donald Brownlee. *Rare Earth: Why Complex Life Is Uncommon in the Universe*. New York: Copernicus Books, softcover edition 2004, first published 2000. Page references are to the softcover edition.

Wikipedia. "Galactic Center," found at
https://en.wikipedia.org/wiki/Galactic_Center, last
edited May 27, 2018 (last viewed May 29, 2018).
———. "Near-Earth supernova," found at
https://en.wikipedia.org/wiki/Near-
Eearth_supernova, last edited June 21, 2018 (last
viewed July 10, 2018).
———. "Oxygen toxicity," found at
https://en.wikipedia.org/wiki/Oxygen_toxicity, last
edited April 10, 2018 (last viewed June 19, 2018).
———. "Ozone layer," found at
https://en.wikipedia.org/wiki/Ozone_layer last updated June 7, 2018 (last viewed June 15, 2018).
———. "Pascal's Wager," found at
https://en.wikipedia.org/wiki/Pascal%27s_Wager (last
viewed 4/5/2018).
———. "Speed of Light," found at
https://en.wikipedia.org/Speed_of_light (last viewed
May 29, 2018).
———. "Tunguska event," found
athttps://en.wikipedia.org/wiki/Tunguska_event, last
edited June 28, 2018 (last viewed June 28, 2018).
"Why is there Life on Earth?: Bob the Alien's Tour of the Solar System," found at
https://www.bobthealien.co.uk/earth/life.htm (last
viewed May 10, 2018).

ABOUT THE AUTHOR

Who I am. As I explained in my first book, *Beyond Blind Faith*, I am a happily married husband of thirty-six years, father of two, and lawyer by trade. I have been a Christian for almost forty-three years. During that time, studying the Bible and Judeo-Christian history has been my hobby, and at times my obsession.

My Spiritual Development. In my first book, I shared my conversion experience when I was twenty years old. If I may backtrack a bit, the semester before I gave my heart to Christ, I read the New Testament as part of a college course on morality. I remember thinking at the time, "What nonsense! How could anyone believe this?"

And then, because of an answered prayer, I became convinced that Christianity was true. So I set about reading the New Testament again, convinced that I was now going to have to change all of my values to fit my new normal. Instead, I was shocked to find that my values were already there, in the New Testament. As I read it, I kept saying to myself, "I've believed this all my life. Why did I never see it before?"

I felt like I was reading a different book. The only explanation I have for this is that the Holy Spirit opened my eyes and my heart to see what was previously hidden. That experience has helped ground my faith on a firm foundation ever since. So did what happened a few years later.

I went on active duty with the U.S. Navy in 1980. The needs of the Navy stationed me in Long Beach, California for the next four-and-a-half years, where I soon began listening to a unique preacher named Dr. Gene Scott,[1] who was then pastor of Faith Center in Glendale, California.

Once a year, Dr. Scott gave a sermon on the historical evidence for the resurrection of Jesus Christ. This was a completely new concept for me—faith grounded in historical fact. As a lawyer, I was intrigued by the idea that faith could be based on objective evidence rather than on mere subjective belief. So I began my own study of the evidence, a study that would eventually serve as the basis for Chapter Two of *Beyond Blind Faith*: "Is Jesus' Resurrection Fact or Fairy Tale?"

Dr. Scott also gave me a new way of looking at the Old Testament, which had proven difficult for me to understand and troubling for my faith. He helped me see that the Old Testament was an effort by God to teach a spiritually immature people to trust Him, much like a parent trying to discipline a toddler. And they were often a disobedient toddler.

Since I had grown up as an agnostic, I had a severe inferiority complex when I became a baby Christian. I assumed that Christians who had grown up in the faith must know the Bible backwards and forwards, so I had a lot of catching up to do. In an effort to cure my ignorance, I resolved to read the Bible for at least five minutes every day—which I did. And I took notes. Pretty soon five minutes was not enough, so I expanded my resolution to ten minutes, and then fifteen. Eventually I was reading the Bible at least thirty minutes a day, and often longer.

---

1. William Eugene Scott, August 14, 1929 – February 21, 2005

One Christmas my wife, Marsha, gave me one of the best presents I have ever received—the Wycliffe Bible commentary. It opened a whole new world of biblical understanding for me. Suddenly passages made sense that had previously seemed confusing or obscure. I later studied additional commentaries and other books, enlarging the foundations of my understanding.

As an introvert at heart, prayer has always been difficult for me, especially praying out loud. I never felt that I was good at it—actually, for a long time I believed I was terrible at it. Only after many years did I come to understand that prayer is not about impressing God, or anyone else, but about communicating with a friend. And I take great comfort in Romans 8:26-27, where Paul promises us that the Spirit will help our inadequacies in that department.

I have studied the lives of many faithful Christians, and the one predominant trait I find in every one of them is humility. The closer they come to God, it seems, the more they realize their own weaknesses, faults, and shortcomings—like how a bright light exposes dust and spider webs that were previously unseen.

Humility reminds us that we all have a long way to go on the path toward spiritual maturity. I certainly do. But my hope is that this book will help both of us get a little further along that path than we were before.

May God bless you, and may you be a blessing to others. (Genesis 12:2-3.)

Don

www.ingramcontent.com/pod-product-compliance
Lightning Source LLC
Chambersburg PA
CBHW031953040426
42448CB00006B/344